The Horse
Grooming Manual

The Horse Grooming Manual

ALISON POCKLINGTON

THE CROWOOD PRESS

First published in 2015 by
The Crowood Press Ltd
Ramsbury, Marlborough
Wiltshire SN8 2HR

www.crowood.com

British Library Cataloguing-in-Publication Data
A catalogue record for this book is available from the British Library.

ISBN 978 1 78500 080 5

Disclaimer
The author and publisher do not accept any responsibility in any manner whatsoever for any error or omission, or any loss, damage, injury, adverse outcome, or liability of any kind incurred as a result of the use of any of the information contained in this book, or reliance upon it.

Frontispiece: Crispin Mould

All photographs are by Matthew Roberts Photographer unless stated otherwise.

Typeset by Jean Cussons Typesetting, Diss, Norfolk

Printed and bound in Malaysia by Times Offset (M) Sdn Bhd

Contents

Introduction

My love of horses started at a very early age. I was a typical pony-mad little girl who wanted to spend every possible moment at the stables. My fondest memories are not of riding and competing but of the time I spent caring for my pony. The hours of grooming, washing, trimming and plaiting to prepare for competitions gave me pleasure and satisfaction. It also built very special relationships with my ponies. The enjoyment I derived from this remains with me and I am fortunate enough to have made a

(Photo: Shannon Daly)

career out of what I love doing – grooming and caring for horses.

Throughout my career, I have had the opportunity to share my knowledge and practical experiences with others, some of whom have gone on to be professional grooms. I take great pride in the fact that I have assisted others in achieving their goals.

There are many aspects of grooming other than the obvious reason of improving the appearance of the horse. This book explores other areas which relate to grooming, such as horse health, horse psychology and basic handling, as well as turning out for competition.

It is a book that all horse owners should be able to relate to, from the pony-mad child to those who ride for pleasure, and will be useful for those who want to learn more about the professional care required to produce healthy horses looking their best for competition and the show ring.

1 Qualities of a Good Horse Owner and Professional Groom

There is nothing more rewarding than forming a great partnership with a horse. This could be a person who rides as a hobby and regards his horse as a friend or a top competition rider or groom working with the horse as a professional. At any level, as a horse owner it is important to understand what is required if the partnership is to become successful. Those who want to take this a step further and make horses their career must be prepared for hard work and long hours. Working with or owning any animal is not a nine-to-five job but often a 24-hour a day commitment.

Below is a summary of what is required of a good horse owner.

The Pony Club gives children a great start. (Photo: Shannon Daly)

- There are many aspects of stable management to be considered before buying a horse. The basics include feeding, mucking out, grooming, horse health, farriery, tack, equipment and exercise. It is necessary to have

Working pupils often learn 'on the job'.

some knowledge on all these subjects. Information can be obtained from reading books, watching DVDs or attending stable management courses. Anyone intending to make a career with horses is advised to look into what exams are available to take, either through the British Horse Society or by attending college full-time. Courses range from basic all the way up to degree level.

● Children who attend the Pony Club are given a fantastic introduction to stable management. The Pony Club exams concentrate on horse care as much as on riding. Those who achieve the higher levels are extremely competent.

● More important than theoretical knowledge is practical experience. Reading about a subject gives an idea of what is expected in caring for a horse but until this is actually practised competence is not achieved. It is a mistake to consider buying a horse if your only previous experience involved turning up for a riding lesson where the horse was tacked up, ready and waiting. If this is the case, try to spend more time on the yard before and after lessons to observe and help with stable duties. The other option is to find a local person with horses and, if possible, help out and gain experience.

- A young person wanting to make a career with horses may choose to become a working pupil rather than go through college. This involves going to work on a yard. The responsibilities should be minimal to begin with, and the working pupil will work with more experienced staff to learn 'on the job'. Formal training will also be received. This often proves to be a more successful route for competition grooms as it opens doors to further employment in the industry.

- Anyone considering owning or working with horses must be prepared for hard work. Unless lucky enough to have a horse on full livery, an owner must be prepared to care for the horse before and after work and at weekends. A career with horses entails long hours and physical effort. This is especially true in the competition and hunting industry.

- Working with a horse requires a person to gain his respect by acting in a calm, firm manner. Horses are big strong animals that can become dangerous if this is not practised. Patience is also required. There is a great saying: 'Always have more time than your horse.' He must learn to trust your leadership without overstepping the line or

A professional groom.

being afraid of you. This is discussed in more depth in the handling chapter.

- Safety is essential. Even the quietest horses can have a scare and revert back to their natural instincts. This book discusses how to work around the horse safely to avoid accidents. This is often forgotten when people become complacent about a horse because they think they know him well.

- Horses thrive on routine and will benefit physically and mentally from it. Therefore it is important to be organized, to plan ahead and have excellent time management skills. This is essential when working with a number of horses and preparing for competition.

- Stress – of the horse or rider – is not conducive to producing good results. A groom's role is to minimize stress at all times. When things do not go to plan it is important not to panic but to remain calm and work through the problem.

- When turning out for competition, it is essential to pay attention to detail and take pride in the work. For a groom or horse owner, seeing the horse in peak condition, and turned out immaculately, is rewarding and what the hard work is all about.

2 Handling

Grooming should be a pleasurable experience for both horse and groom. Done well, grooming aids bonding, helping to build trust and confidence, which will, it is hoped, contribute to a great partnership. This is especially important for competition horses that will often be stabled away from home in a strange environment and yet still be expected to perform to a high standard. Taking a horse away from everything he is familiar with can often cause stress and anxiety. This can be minimized if he knows and trusts his groom and rider.

A good partnership is equally important for those who ride for pleasure. In the end, someone who buys a horse for a hobby is also expecting to enjoy the time spent with him.

When dealing with an older, more experienced horse, his basic manners are often taken for granted. It is easy to forget that the horse was not born knowing how to react to the everyday things that are part of his daily routine. At some point he had to be introduced to a halter, trained to lead and tie up, have strange equipment used over his body, legs and head. He had to learn to balance on three legs while people did things to his other foot. He had to accept a hosepipe, buckets and sponges being used to wash him. Knowledgeable handling ensures that his good manners remain consistent.

A poor introduction to these things will result in the horse being nervous of the experience, which often leads to bad behaviour. This chapter explores how to introduce handling and grooming, which, it is hoped, will result in a well-mannered, confident horse who enjoys the experience. It will also discuss reasons for bad behaviour and how this can be managed.

HORSE BEHAVIOUR

In order to handle horses well it is important to have some knowledge and understanding of their natural behaviour.

The horse is a prey animal, meaning that in the wild he would be vulnerable to attack from predatory animals. The horse's reaction to fear or threat is flight, but he may fight if put in a situation or environment where flight is not an option. This behaviour is displayed by biting, kicking, striking out or rearing.

In addition, horses are herd animals. In the wild they live in groups and help protect one another. It is therefore unnatural for a horse to be separated and expected to live and be ridden alone. Often a domesticated horse has to learn to cope with this. A one-horse owner, for example, may have a stable at home rather than keeping the horse at livery on a large yard. Competition horses are often required to leave a working-in area and perform in an arena away from other horses. If the initial separation is not done sympathetically, and the horse allowed time to adjust, it can often cause him distress and negatively shape his behaviour for the rest of his life. Being methodical and building his confidence steadily with correct training will reduce the chances of him being 'herd bound'.

Young horses benefit from company when introduced to new situations.

In the wild horses live in small groups that usually consist of a mature male, several females and their offspring. Within the group exists a hierarchy often referred to as the pecking order. This is also seen in domesticated horses living out in a field together. When a horse first interacts with a human, it is important that he quickly learns to respect the person as being higher in the pecking order than him. Failure to do so will result in him displaying difficult or threatening behaviour when he is handled. This often occurs if a person feels threatened by the horse and shows signs of fear, enabling the horse to become dominant. Experienced, confident handling is essential in the early stages to prevent this from happening. Once the horse has accepted the pecking order, he usually retains

Good handling gains respect.

this throughout his life, provided handling is consistent.

Most young horses do not regard people as a threat, and therefore will not become aggressive without reason. A natural reaction in a young horse would be to try to avoid human contact. Correct handling in the right environment will build up trust, but impatient and aggressive handling at any stage may have the opposite effect. A horse put in a situation where he can't flee from his fear may resort to aggression. Once learnt, such behaviour can often stay with him for the rest of his life.

Good handling comes from a combination of confidence, calmness and patience. The horse must respect the human as dominant without being afraid.

BODY LANGUAGE

The horse communicates mostly through body language, using his ears, eyes, lips, muzzle, legs and tail. Learning to recognize how the horse is feeling and anticipating his likely reaction to certain situations is essential in training the horse, building his trust and developing a partnership. It also helps to ensure the horse is safe to be around and can be taken to places where there will be other horses.

Ears

The ears give several different signs as to how the horse is feeling. As horses have very acute hearing, the ears can often change in a split second.

Pricked ears show that the horse has heard or seen something. He will hold his head high and turn to face the sound, pointing the ears as far forward as they will go. He may become quite tense in his stance until he has worked out what the noise is and is happy there is no threat. Then he will relax again. This 'pointing' stance is also a result of the horse's vision. He uses the lower part of his eyes to view things far away, hence must raise his head to look towards the horizon. When looking at something close, he will often draw the head in and down, using the upper part of his eyes to look at it.

Pinned back ears are a sign of aggression or discomfort. It is a clear warning sign that people and fellow horses should respect and

An inquisitive young horse.

learn to deal with. A horse may feel threatened by another horse coming too close to him, especially when he is eating. He may fear other horses as a result of being kicked or bitten. Mares often dislike others coming too close to them when they are not in season.

If a horse pins back his ears when approached in the stable, it is because he feels threatened in some way and he may revert back to 'fight or flight'. As it is difficult to flee when surrounded by four walls and a door, he may think his only option is to fight. It is important in this situation to establish the pecking order as the horse's behaviour will become worse if he remains dominant. The horse should be disciplined in a firm but calm manner. Shouting at him or threatening him will only cause him further anxiety and is likely to result in him becoming more aggressive.

If the horse lays his ears back when being groomed or tacked up, it is often a sign of discomfort or the expectation of pain because it has been painful in the past. It is important to assess why he is reacting in such a way and wherever possible to remove or treat the cause. It may be that such behaviour has simply become habitual and means no harm; he is simply saying he would rather not have the girth done up. In this case a calm approach to build up his confidence is more appropriate than reprimanding him.

Moving his ears shows the horse is semi-relaxed. He will do this during exercise or while in the stable or field, especially if he is lying down, as he will feel more vulnerable. Although he is quite happy, he is still alert and listening for sounds around him. When the horse is being ridden, the ears move frequently as the horse not only pays attention to his surroundings but also listens to the rider's voice and aids.

Loppy ears show the horse is totally relaxed. He will drop his head and neck and the ears will fall more to the sides. This is often seen when

The horse holds his head high, ears pricked, and turns to face the sound.

This horse's ears show that his concentration is no longer on the handler but on something to the side.

This horse is curious but does not feel threatened.

a horse is dozing in the stable or paddock. It shows he is confident in his surroundings and not at all worried.

Eyes

Horses' eyes vary in size and in their placement on the head. It is often said that a horse with a larger eye has a kind eye, while one with small eyes looks unfriendly. The size and shape of the eye can be an indicator of demeanour. When the horse is relaxed, the eyes tend to look softer, giving him a kinder look. A horse showing signs of fear or aggression will often show the whites of his eyes, giving a more feral look.

Mouth

The mouth is a good indicator of disposition at any given time. When the horse is very relaxed, the bottom lip will often droop and hang down. The horse tightens his lips when he is nervous about a situation. The top lip may also become pointed. When working the horse loose, one of the first signs of submission is relaxation of the jaw and licking the lips.

In the wild horses use their lips and teeth to groom one another. They stand face to face and scratch the neck and body. This is a trait that remains strong in the domesticated horse, and some horses may try to reciprocate when being groomed by a human. Observe the horse's face when you are using the curry comb. If he enjoys the experience he may stretch his lips and move them about. If allowed, he may turn his head and neck to make contact by nuzzling with his lips on the person's back or legs. For him this is mutual grooming. This is totally acceptable and a wonderful way of bonding with the horse, although care should be taken as he may also use his teeth. This must not be punished as it is a natural reaction. To avoid it, tie the horse up shorter.

Teeth grinding and biting

Some horses show their anxiety or irritation by grinding their teeth, often with their ears back and tail swishing. It can happen both in hand and during exercise, and a common cause is the horse not being able to tolerate certain aspects of grooming, rugging or tacking up. This may be because he is sensitive and ticklish in certain

A horse looking happy and relaxed.

A horse showing tight lips.

areas, or because he is in pain or associates pain with what is being done. The latter commonly arises when a horse has had an injury or problem and is expecting a certain action still to cause pain to a particular area. It can often take a long time for the horse to forget something that has previously hurt him and regain his trust.

If teeth grinding is ignored, the horse may go one step further and snap with his teeth. Some do this in a threatening manner but without trying to make contact, but others will bite. This must be taken seriously and will be discussed later.

Tail swishing

The horse swishes his tail as a warning signal or to show he is irritated by something. The most common cause of tail swishing is to discourage flies and should never be reprimanded.

Tail swishing may also occur if another horse comes too close. If the second horse chooses to ignore the warning, he is in danger of being kicked. The same may apply to people. The horse may find grooming, clipping, pulling the mane and tail or tacking up annoying, ticklish or painful. The areas that tend to be most sensitive are around the girth, belly and hind legs. His way of saying 'I don't think I can tolerate this' is to swish his tail. If this is ignored, he may then kick. It is important to assess why he is reacting in such a way before deciding how to deal with it.

High tail carriage

A horse often carries his tail high in the air if something has alerted him. It is a sign of fear or excitement triggered by noise, spooking or other animals. Raising his head and neck, he may stop and freeze or his

This horse is ticklish around his girth area and his body language shows he is not happy.

steps may become very elevated. He may also stop and snort. He should be given time to assess the situation before pressure is applied. Firm but calm handling will reassure and settle him.

Tail clamped

The horse will clamp his tail as a reaction to fear or pain. If he suddenly gets a fright from behind, he clamps his tail and shoots

This horse is worried about the situation. His tail carriage is high and he has frozen in his step.

The handler is calm and gives the horse time to assess the situation.

This horse is clamping his tail as the bandage is applied.

Horses can kick out behind them or cow kick by bringing the leg forwards. If a horse swings his quarters to the stable door in response to someone entering, it is a sign that he is worried about this invasion into his personal space. The stable must never be entered with a horse positioned this way. He has attempted to flee, but he can't as there is no way out so instead he may resort to fight and may strike out with his hind legs. Remaining outside the stable, encourage him to turn to face the door before entering. Reward him when he does so.

If the horse is standing with his quarters to the door, unaware that someone is about to enter, he may get a fright when the door opens and instinctively kick out. This is not a sign of aggression: he is simply protecting himself. Always speak to the horse before entering the stable, so he is not taken by surprise.

When the horse is being groomed or handled, he will usually swish his tail as a warning that he is not happy with a situation. If this signal is ignored, he may lift a hind leg or stamp a foot before actually kicking. As discussed, always assess what may be causing the problem and avoid it if possible. If flies are annoying the horse, he is more likely to cow kick to try to dislodge them. He should not be reprimanded for this. If possible, move him to an area where the flies are not such a problem, and apply fly repellent.

forward. He may also clamp his tail when having his dock sponged or a tail bandage applied. This is a warning sign that he is not comfortable with what is being done, and if the warning is not acted on, he may kick out. More time should be taken brushing his tail and gently lifting the dock to give him confidence.

The horse may also clamp his tail if he is cold. This can often be seen at the start of exercise when being ridden in cold weather.

Kicking with the hind legs

The horse may kick with his hind legs in response to fright, aggression or irritation.

Forelegs

The horse may paw or stamp the ground with a foreleg, either in the stable at feed times or when he is tied up for grooming. This is a sign of impatience or irritation, and should be discouraged as it can become a bad habit. Pawing at feed time can develop into door kicking, which is both annoying and not good for the legs or the door. Pawing when tied up may lead to striking out.

Flies may also cause the horse to stamp.

If a horse is seen to be pawing when he is loose in the stable or field it could be a sign of discomfort, and is often associated with colic.

The horse may also strike out with a foreleg if he feels threatened and can't flee, or if he wants to assert his dominance. This behaviour is often displayed by stallions. It is important to correct it immediately and an experienced and confident person is required to handle the horse using the correct equipment such as a bridle or chiffney. Failure to do so could lead to rearing, putting the handler in danger.

EARLY HANDLING

The earlier a horse is handled and introduced to grooming, the more likely he is to accept it and not worry about the process. It is a great advantage if a foal is handled from birth. At this stage he may be timid, but will be more inquisitive than afraid. A foal learns and gains confidence from his mother, so her attitude towards human contact may influence him. Studies have shown that foals become more trusting of people when they see their mothers being handled well in the first few days after birth, rather than the foals themselves being handled.

Calm steady handling reassures the nervous horse. This is shown on his facial expression.

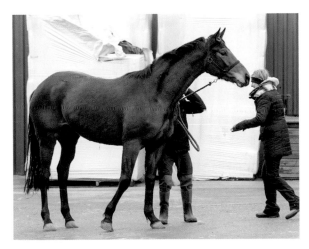

The young horse benefits from frequent handling.

The horse must learn to yield to pressure on the rope.

If a foal is left unhandled until he is weaned, his fight or flight instinct will be much stronger. Not only has he to deal with the trauma of being separated from his mother, he also has to cope with unfamiliar human contact. He may not yet be mature and strong but his quick athletic movements will make him very tricky to handle. Using a forced method will cause fear or panic and can often lead to injury. A bad experience at this time is likely to stay with him for life.

Once weaned, most youngsters are turned away in groups, where they thrive physically and mentally. Racehorses may start their careers as yearlings or two-year-olds but most other horses don't start until they are at least two or three years old. During this maturing period it is advantageous if regular handling continues. Keeping the horse in his comfort zone will help him to accept being handled and groomed and to tolerate visits from the farrier. He will be much more settled if he remains in the company of other horses. Don't suddenly take him away from the others and put him into a strange stable as this will probably lead to trouble. The more familiar he becomes with human contact, the more his confidence and respect will develop, making it much easier to separate him from other horses when the time comes.

TYING UP

It is important to teach any horse to tie up and stand patiently and remain relaxed. If this is done badly in the beginning, he may always object to the idea and continue to resist, making handling and working around him frustrating and often unsafe.

A horse that pulls back when he is tied up and ends up in a struggle against the rope can do himself serious harm. His neck and back will suffer from the force of the pull, and he may even end up falling or being flung

Always tie to string.

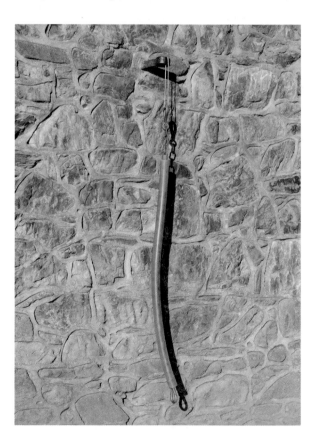

A quick release rope can be used.

back when the rope snaps, leading to more serious injury.

Before attempting to tie up a young horse, especially for the first time, it is essential that he is happy wearing a headcollar and has had some introduction to pressure on the rope. He must have learnt to yield to the pressure and not resist it. Choose a suitable, safe location where the horse will be relaxed and unlikely to harm himself. Avoid taking him away from other horses and familiar surroundings. A non-slip surface such as dirt, straw or rubber matting is much safer than concrete.

The tie-up ring should be at a suitable height, which is no lower than the horse's withers. Once the horse has been trained, and doesn't pull back, it is common practice to tie a small loop of bale string into the ring. The horse's rope can then be tied to the string rather than to the ring. In an emergency, if the horse does get a fright and panics, the string will break, freeing him without too much of a struggle. String should not be used when initially training the horse to tie up as all too often youngsters learn that without too much effort they can pull back and free themselves. If this becomes a habit, the horse can not safely be left tied up.

To begin with, thread the rope through the ring and hold the free end in one hand. A longer lead rope is useful for this. With the other hand, gently touch the horse's neck, body and legs until he is standing still and

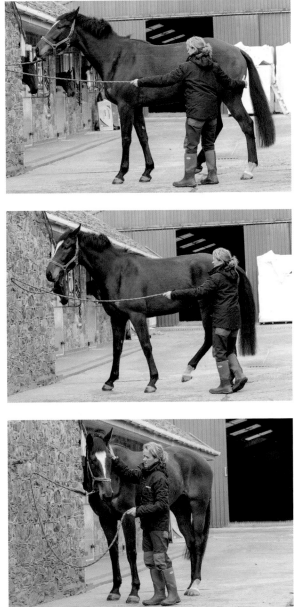

The rope is placed through the ring and held on to.

The horse feels the pressure and wants to go backwards. The handler releases the pressure, encourages him to step forwards and then rewards.

happy with this. If the horse goes to move back, he will feel the pressure on the rope; this is what causes him to panic and pull against it, especially if halter training has not been properly established. He must learn to release the pressure by stepping forward. If possible, stand slightly behind him and encourage this with the voice and hand. Care must be taken not to get kicked. If the horse doesn't immediately respond in the correct way, release the pressure by giving him more rope. This process must be repeated until he gets the idea. Sometimes a second handler may be required to assist.

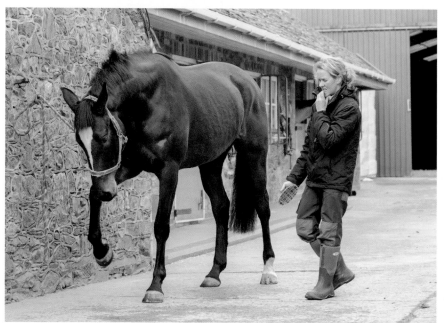

The young horse shows signs of impatience. This can be caused by the grooming session being too long.

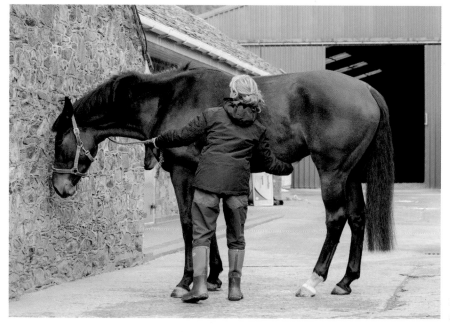

The horse learns to relax as the handler works around him.

Eventually the horse can be tied up.

COMMON MISTAKES

- Using an unsuitable area with a slippery surface, resulting in the horse falling over.
- Equipment left lying around, causing the area to be unsafe.
- Taking the horse away from familiar surroundings and other horses.
- Insufficient halter training before attempting to tie up.
- Using the wrong equipment.
- Tying the horse to the string loop too soon so he learns how to pull back and snap it.
- Training the horse on an elastic rope, allowing the horse to swing off it and throw himself around, often resulting in injury.
- If the tie ring is too low, the horse can put his foot over the rope.
- Using an unsuitable rope. If the rope is too long, the horse may get his foot over the rope or the rope may become caught over his head; both may cause him to panic. If the rope is too short, it may cause too much pressure and discomfort, causing him to resist.
- Leaving the horse tied up for too long in the early stages.
- Tying the horse to unsafe structures. Always use a solid post or fixed tie-up ring. Common features around the yard that may look strong but should be avoided include doors, gates, rails and bars on windows.
- Failing to use a quick release knot.

When the horse has reached the stage where he is happy to stand with the rope through the ring, start to move further away from him and increase the length of time he is standing there. A haynet will help him relax and prevent him getting bored during these sessions. If he shows signs of anxiety when he is left alone, regularly reassure him or try standing an older, quieter horse next to him. Regular short sessions several times a day are more valuable than one long session. Make it a habit to put on his headcollar and stand him at the tie ring when doing any small jobs such as skipping out or changing a rug.

Once the horse is happy and relaxed, the rope can be attached to the string loop using a quick release knot. To begin with, work quietly around the horse and do not move too far away from him. Avoid introducing anything new at this stage and always untie him if attempting to do something he is unsure about. Never try to do anything around his head when the horse is tied up. Once the horse is confident, introduce him to different tie-up areas around the yard.

An alternative method is to use a training rope in the early stages. The training rope has a clip that is designed to allow the horse some relief when he feels the pressure, without actually breaking free.

PICKING UP THE FEET

Picking up the feet is an essential part of a horse's education. Without this, it is impossible to check their condition or clean them, and it can make life very difficult for the farrier. The sooner the training is introduced, the easier it will be. Safety is paramount.

At first the horse will not understand the question and is likely to feel threatened by the action as standing on three legs inhibits his ability to flee. Some horses may also feel discomfort when a foot is picked up; this is more obvious if one particular limb is more difficult than the others.

It is essential that the handler is both confident and competent. It is very easy to feel

This horse is tied up too long.

This horse is tied too short but this is appropriate to prevent biting.

The area is unsafe, with equipment lying around too close to the horse.

An unsafe structure and area to tie up.

threatened if the horse is resisting and there is a danger of being kicked. The horse will soon recognize that he has the upper hand should the handler not remain calm and in control, and the task will become more difficult.

The horse should be well handled and confident with his legs and feet being touched. Choose a suitable environment where the horse is relaxed. A good-sized stable will offer a non-slip floor and prevent the horse moving about too much.

Initially, have a handler to assist rather than

Picking up the feet should be introduced at an early stage.

tying up the horse. Most horses are happier being handled on the left side rather than the right, so start with the near fore. Run a hand down the horse's neck, shoulder and forearm to the lower leg. Slightly squeeze the leg and the horse may react by picking up the foot. If he does, release it and praise him. Don't try to hold on at this stage and don't try to alter the position of the foot. Repeat the process until the horse's natural reaction is to pick up the foot when he feels the pressure. Once the horse has got the hang of one leg, move on to the next. If he shows any signs of stress or impatience, give him a break and try again later.

If pressure alone does not get a reaction, try leaning against the shoulder to shift the weight off the leg. Alternately, squeezing the chestnut often causes him to pick up the foot.

If the horse is objecting and not getting the idea, an alternative method is to use a soft rope. Standing in front of the horse, place the rope under his fetlock and gently pull to encourage him to lift the leg. When he complies, reward him by allowing the foot back to the ground. Repeat until he happily picks up the foot, and then try again using the hand.

If the horse repeatedly objects to one particular foot being picked up, it is likely that it is physically difficult for him to do so. Rather than try to force the issue and upset the horse, it is advisable to have a vet check him over.

Some horses may react in the opposite manner and be very sharp with their legs, stamping and kicking. This can put the handler at risk. In such a case, the horse needs to be made less sensitive to his legs being touched. The safest way to do this is to use a long stick covered in a towel. Standing in a safe place, run the stick gently up and down the legs until the horse no longer feels threatened by his legs been touched.

A rope can be used to encourage the horse to pick up the foot.

SAFETY TIPS FOR PICKING UP THE FEET

- Start picking up feet at an early age and regularly repeat the process.
- Don't attempt to pick up feet unless confident at doing so.
- Ensure the horse is well handled and happy to have his feet and legs touched.
- Choose a safe environment with a non-slip floor, clear of hazards.
- Wear suitable footwear and other protective clothing if necessary.
- Always stand in a safe place to reduce the chance of being kicked.
- Take it step by step and never hurry the horse.

GENERAL SAFETY TIPS

- Have a good knowledge of equine body language.
- Observe the horse closely at all times and react accordingly to his body language.
- Do not attempt a task unless fully confident and competent to carry it out.
- Always seek help if unsure.
- Always let the horse know when approaching him from behind.
- Horses may feel threatened if approached head on. Always go to the shoulder first.
- Horses can initially feel threatened by direct eye contact.
- Never make contact with the hindquarters first. A surprise pat may cause him to kick out as he instinctively tries to defend himself.
- Always start at the shoulder and move forward or back to the area requiring attention.
- Never walk directly behind an unfamiliar horse or lead another horse past too closely.
- Don't stand directly behind the horse when grooming the tail and hind legs.
- Never sit or kneel next to the horse; always crouch.
- Tie the horse up to deal with him. This prevents him from developing bad manners.
- Always wear correct clothing and footwear.
- When working with the horse, converse with him without shouting. He will learn to recognize the different tones of voice used to calm, reward or reprimand.

WORKING SAFELY AROUND HORSES

Before attempting to handle and work around horses it is important to have some knowledge of safety factors to help prevent accidents. Horses are big and strong, and even quiet, well mannered ones can be unpredictable at times. Young or nervous horses obviously need more expertise and respect.

Never stand directly in front of the foreleg.

Standing directly behind a horse is extremely dangerous.

Avoid standing in front of the horse to examine his mouth.

BONDING

Like humans, horses have different personalities. Some are nervous where others are bold; some are independent and like their own space where others like company and thrive on attention. In order to bond with the horse and develop a partnership, it is important to respect his character. It is unlikely that a horse who appears anti-social will suddenly change into a loving, friendly creature. However, his attitude may change if he is allowed his personal space and not fussed over more than necessary. The most important thing is that the horse respects his handler and accepts what needs to be done. This should be reciprocated by the handler. Mutual respect is paramount.

Temperament is an important consideration when buying a horse. Usually the one-horse owner or amateur rider will want to spend more time with the horse and will derive as much pleasure from caring for him as from riding him. Often the horse is treated more like a pet dog would be. A horse that doesn't enjoy being groomed and pampered would not suit this role and the owner may become frustrated, making it difficult to build a partnership.

Professional riders tend to have less time to spend on the ground with their horses and often it is the job of a groom to care for them. The temperament is less important as the horse's main role is performing in competition. Competition grooms should have the knowledge and experience to deal with more complex characters, and a mutual respect can develop.

A partnership develops when the horse is confident and trusting. One thing that all horses thrive on is routine, knowing what is going to happen when. If a routine is maintained on a daily basis, trust will develop more easily. Horses tend to appreciate being handled by one person rather than by lots of different people. On large competition yards grooms tend to have certain horses in their care and try not to swap around too much. It is as beneficial for the groom to know each horse as it is for the horse to know his groom.

If the horse enjoys the attention of grooming and trimming, as much time as possible should be spent doing this to enhance the relationship. If the horse doesn't enjoy the experience, then try to minimize it and only do what is necessary to keep him clean and healthy. He may be happier out of the stable and enjoy time hand-grazing.

For me, there is nothing more rewarding than the feeling that the horse respects and trusts you, and enjoys the work that is put into him.

INTRODUCING THE HORSE TO GROOMING

Early introduction to grooming will benefit the horse in many ways. A foal will gain confidence by standing by his mother while she is groomed, handled or has her feet dealt with. The more interaction he encounters, the more relaxed he will be when his turn comes.

Before attempting to put a brush over the

The horse is first shown the stable rubber.

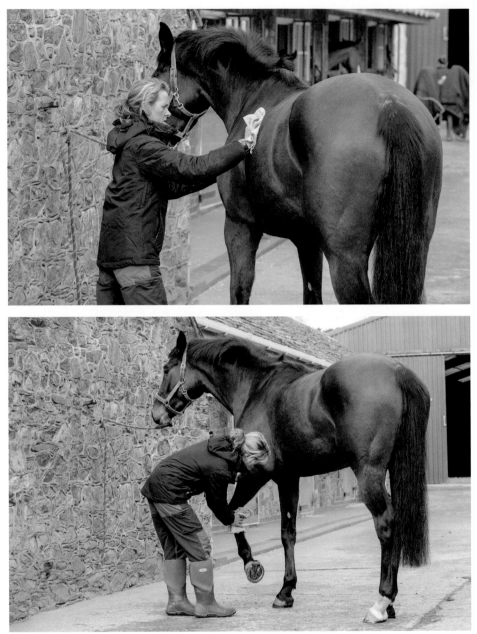

The horse must get used to the feel of the cloth over his body and legs.

horse, he must be well acquainted with hands touching him all over, including his legs. This process will make it very clear if the horse objects to being touched in certain areas. This is usually a sign that he is ticklish, or perhaps feels vulnerable. Repetition and reward will build up his confidence.

Introduce the grooming process with a soft cloth folded into the shape of a body brush. Show it to the horse first, giving him time to look and smell. Once he is happy, start at the shoulder and gently rub the cloth over him, always in the direction of the hair. Slowly work over his neck, back and hindquarters, reassuring him all the time and avoiding areas he is not happy with. Initially, do not make the sessions

Next the body brush is introduced.

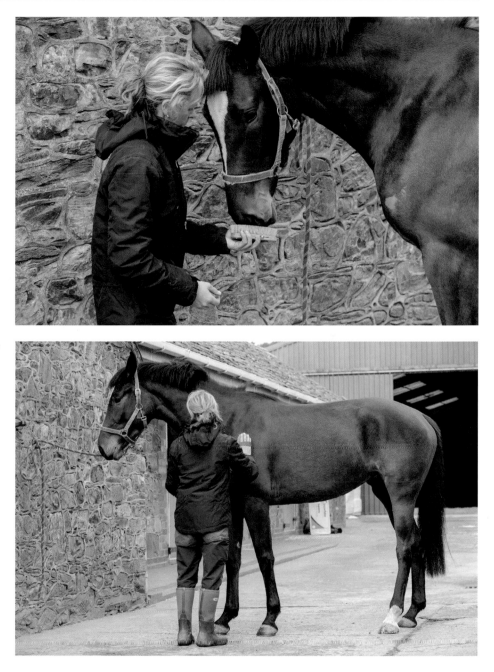

Introducing the body brush. The handler keeps a close eye on the horse's reaction.

too long. It is better to stop while the horse is happy than to go on for too long, which may turn into a bad experience. Repeat with the cloth until he is happy to have his body, legs and head done.

Next a soft brush can be introduced. Again show it to the horse first and then repeat the process used with the cloth. A metal curry comb can be used to clean the brush. The noise may alarm the horse to begin with, and avoid banging it on the wall or ground too close to him as this may also startle him.

As the horse becomes more confident, different grooming utensils can be introduced,

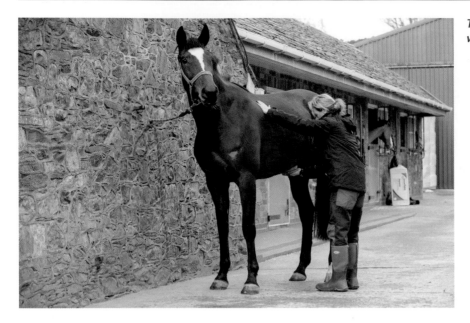

The horse looks happy with the procedure.

and the mane, tail and feet included in the routine.

It will soon become clear what the horse's attitude is towards grooming, what areas he likes or dislikes, and which utensils he prefers and those he cannot tolerate. Try to work with him in the early stages to build up trust and tolerance in areas where he is sensitive. In doing so, he will gradually begin to realize that grooming is a pleasurable experience and nothing to worry about.

BAD BEHAVIOUR WHEN GROOMING

Unfortunately, not all horses enjoy being groomed. If the horse is in pain, or the action of grooming is causing him some discomfort, he may display this by trying to move away or pulling back. Alternately if he feels he cannot get away then he may threaten by putting his ears back, grinding his teeth and swishing his tail. If this is ignored, he may bite or kick.

Some horses are sensitive or ticklish. The most commonly affected areas are the girth area, back, belly and lower legs. The horse will display the same body language as when in pain.

Horses that have been poorly handled in the past, or have been punished for not behaving whilst being groomed, may become defensive. This may also be the case if they have experienced pain in the past and associate it with grooming.

Be sure to use the correct equipment. Finer coated horses, such as thoroughbreds, often can't tolerate stiffer brushes or curry combs. The same may apply to a horse with a clipped coat. Not recognizing this may lead to the horse objecting to grooming.

Lastly, the horse has to be happy and relaxed if he is to enjoy the grooming session. Trying to groom in unfamiliar surroundings can make him unsettled and nervous, causing him to move around a lot, stamping and calling to his friends. This makes grooming hard work and an unpleasant experience for all.

Dealing with badly behaved horses

A horse that exhibits bad manners when being groomed makes the task more difficult and may be at risk of injuring himself or the groom. He must learn to accept the essential aspects of grooming to maintain good health and turnout, although he may never grow to enjoy it.

Try to identify exactly what is causing the bad behaviour and, if possible, eliminate the reason. Often this will not have an immediate effect, as the horse needs to build up trust and confidence that he is no longer going to feel pain, sensitivity or threat.

It is important to avoid accidents. Always choose a safe working environment, and always tie up the horse. A smaller space will limit how much he can move about.

A horse that threatens to bite should be tied very short. When grooming in an area where he can reach to bite, hold the headcollar at the side of his head. If he still threatens to bite, raise the hand and reprimand him with your voice, but NEVER hit him on the head. When he moves away, reward him with a pat. In severe cases a muzzle should be applied. Cross-tying can also limit the movement of his head and control how much he can move around.

If the horse threatens to kick, be very aware of this when working around the belly and hindquarters. Speak firmly to him if he threatens to kick, and back this up with a sharp tap of the hand if necessary. This is only effective if the timing is correct: the action must immediately follow the horse's threat if he

A muzzle can be worn to prevent biting.

is to relate the two things together. Shouting and smacking him thirty seconds later will only cause him to become more defensive. An assistant may be required to hold up a front leg.

The horse must not be allowed to dominate and he must accept what has to be done. In return, the job should be done as efficiently as possible.

3 The Grooming Kit

There are numerous items available to buy for the grooming kit, and the choice largely depends on the required result. For example, a horse that is used for pleasure will require a basic grooming kit that contains the essential equipment to keep the horse healthy and presentable. A competition horse will require more specific equipment to produce a much higher standard of turnout.

This chapter lists the items of the grooming kit and explains when, where and how to use them.

HOOF PICK

The hoof pick is used to pick out and clean the inside of the hoof in order to keep the foot healthy and prevent lameness. The condition of the foot and shoes should also be checked at the same time. Introducing picking out the feet is discussed in Chapter 2.

Hoof pick.

The feet should be picked out at least once a day and for the following:

- Before leaving the stable. This enables the feet and shoes to be checked before exercise or turning out. It also prevents bedding and muck being deposited across the yard.
- Before exercise.
- After exercise. When the horse has been working in an arena or field, surface mud can often become packed hard into the hoof. Failure to remove this may lead to the development of thrush, a bacterial condition of the foot.
- When checking the horse in the field.
- When the horse is brought in from the field.

To begin, the horse should be standing on a non-slip surface, relaxed and paying attention to the handler. It is not always necessary to have the horse tied up if he is familiar with the procedure and has good manners, but he should not be allowed to lower his head to eat as this may distract him and may also throw him off balance, causing him to pull the foot away.

Always start with a foreleg. Stand at the horse's shoulder, facing the tail, with the hoof pick in the hand furthest away from the horse. Run the other hand down the back of the leg from the knee to the pastern. Experienced horses will recognize this movement and automatically lift the foot. If the horse resists, check to see if he is standing in good balance. If it is a lack of understanding, apply more pressure and at the same time lean your body weight against the horse's shoulder. This slightly changes their balance, often causing them to shift more weight onto the opposite leg, making it easier to pick up the foot. Once lifted, hold it up with your hand under the hoof. The foot may be packed with bedding, mud or arena surface. Both the latter can be difficult to remove. Stones may also be mixed in and can often cause bruising and lameness if not picked out.

To be effective, the hoof pick must be sharp. Having an understanding of the structure of the foot and knowing what parts are sensitive will reduce the risk of causing damage to the foot with the hoof pick. The frog is a sensitive structure and care must be taken with it. The hoof pick should be used in the direction of heel to toe, loosening and removing the muck from the foot. The cleft that runs beside the frog can often be very deep and it is important to do a thorough job.

ILLUSTRATION STRUCTURE OF THE FOOT

Once the hoof is clean, assess the condition of the foot and shoe before gently lowering the

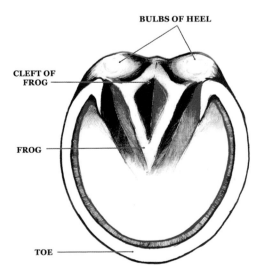

foot to the ground. Then move on to the hind leg on the same side. Again give the horse some warning of your intention by running the inside hand down the leg from the hock. The hind leg may not be as easy and care should be taken not to get kicked. Try not to hold the foot too high as this may cause the horse discomfort and he may resist more. The hoof can be picked out in the same manner. Continue the procedure for all four hooves.

RUBBER CURRY COMB

The rubber curry comb is an essential item of the grooming kit. Its main purpose is to remove loose hair and dried sweat and bring grease

Rubber curry comb.

to the surface of the coat. It can be used to remove mud but is not the most effective tool for doing so. There are many variations of the rubber curry comb available, all doing a similar job. Selection is a matter of personal preference.

The rubber curry comb can be used on most areas. Some horses enjoy the experience, while others do not tolerate it as well, especially on more sensitive or ticklish areas, such as under the belly. It is most effective on larger surface

Structure of the foot. (Diagram: Rozalia Szatanik)

areas, such as the neck, back and hindquarters. It can be used on the face and upper legs with care, but avoid using it on the lower legs. Clipped horses are often more sensitive to it.

The horse should be tied up and rugs removed or quartered back in cold weather. The coat needs to be dry. The curry comb is used in a circular motion, starting at the shoulder. Once the horse is familiar with it, move on to the neck area, then work back towards the tail, sticking to each area until the loose hair stops coming out and fresh grease doesn't appear. If the horse shows signs of discomfort, such as threatening to bite or kick, try using less pressure until he accepts it. Some horses are too sensitive to tolerate it and with them it is best avoided. Shedding hair will be visibly coming away and the curry comb can be regularly banged on the wall or floor to remove it. Grease can be seen on finer coats; this is removed later with the body brush.

PLASTIC CURRY COMB

The plastic curry comb is not an essential item of the grooming kit but can be quite useful. It can be used to brush the mane and tail. It is effective on the mane but can cause damage to the tail as it will often pull out a lot of hair, especially if the tail is very tangled. It is, however, useful for removing mud from the mane and the top of the tail.

The plastic curry comb can also be used for the same purpose as the rubber curry comb and more sensitive horses tend to prefer it. Start at the shoulder and use short strokes in the direction of the hair. Then use on the neck and work back towards the tail. It is effective in removing dry mud and loose hair but doesn't bring the grease to the surface as well as the rubber curry comb. It can be used on all areas of the horse but again care should be taken on the face, legs and ticklish areas.

METAL CURRY COMB

The metal curry comb is an essential item of the grooming kit and is used to clean the loose hair and grease from the body brush during grooming.

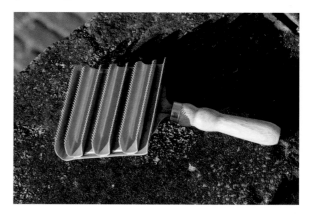

Metal curry comb.

The body brush is held in the hand closest to the horse and the metal curry comb in the other. Following every one to three strokes of the body brush, scrape the curry comb down the bristles of the body brush. The grease and hair can be removed from the curry comb by banging it on the floor or wall.

Plastic curry comb.

DANDY BRUSH

The dandy brush is an essential item of the grooming kit. It is especially useful if the horse is living out or spending time in the field. It is a wooden-backed brush with stiff bristles, used for removing mud and dirt from the coat. The dandy brush should only be used on non-sensitive areas such as the neck, shoulder, body and hindquarters. It may be used on the upper part of the legs but the lower leg and head should be avoided. Horses that are clipped or have fine coats may find the bristles too severe. It should never be used on the tail as it will pull out the hair.

Dandy brush.

Introduce the brush at the shoulder and assess how comfortable the horse is with the firmness of the bristles. Use short strokes following the direction of the hair. If the horse is happy to tolerate it, move to the neck and work backwards to the tail.

BODY BRUSH

The body brush is an essential item of the grooming kit. It is used on the stabled horse to remove dirt and grease from the coat, mane and tail.

Many different body brushes are available in various materials, shapes and sizes. As it is a frequently used item, it is essential to select the most suitable one for horse and groom. The bristles can vary in texture, with some being much softer than others, and this should be taken into account. If the horse has a very thick coat, body brushes with softer bristles may not work well enough. A firmer bristle, though, may be too much for a thin-skinned horse with a fine coat. Using the body brush is quite a strenuous activity, so finding the most comfortable brush to work with is important.

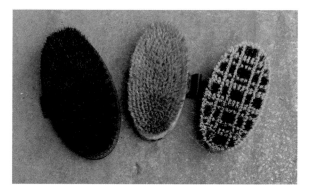

A selection of body brushes.

The body brush can be applied to all areas of the horse, and should be used after heavy mud has been removed from the coat and the grease has been brought to the surface. Start at the neck, facing the tail, with the body brush in the hand closest to the horse and the metal curry comb in the other. Work back from the head to the tail using long strokes on larger areas and smaller strokes on small areas, always following the direction of the hair. Regularly clean the brush with the curry comb. It is also important to feel the condition of the skin and coat as often problems are hidden by the hair. The mane and tail can be brushed by separating and brushing down to the roots. If the horse is brushed daily for twenty minutes, the condition of the skin will improve and the coat will develop an attractive, healthy shine.

FACE BRUSH

The face brush is not an essential item of the grooming kit as the body brush can be used to groom the head. A smaller version of the body brush, with softer bristles, it is less alarming for horses who are head shy and not keen on having their faces brushed.

Face brush.

WATER BRUSH

The water brush is an essential part of the grooming kit. It is similar in design to the dandy brush but the bristles are much softer. Its purpose is to keep the mane and tail neat and tidy. At the end of a grooming session the brush is dipped in water and the mane brushed over to the correct side of the neck. Similarly it can be used for wetting the mane for plaiting. It is also useful on the tail to tidy the appearance or dampen before applying a tail bandage.

The water brush is also useful when bathing the horse, especially for the removal of stable stains. Scrubbing the coat with the soft bristles is more effective at removing grease and stains than using a sponge. There are some water brushes that have a sponge in the centre of the bristles, combining the two.

FLICKY BRUSH

The flicky brush is not an essential item but it is very useful. It is a relatively soft brush like the body brush but the bristles are much longer. It does not remove grease from the coat as effectively as the body brush but it is quick and easy to use when giving the horse a brush-off to make him tidy and presentable for riding. The brush can be used on all areas of the horse with short strokes following the direction of the hair.

Flicky brush.

HOOF BRUSH

Another essential item of the grooming kit, the hoof brush is a hard-bristled brush that is used to scrub the inside and outside of the hoof. This is an important procedure to maintain a healthy foot and suitable appearance for competition.

A dandy brush or a household scrubbing brush are both suitable for the job. Scrubbing the feet should be done at least twice a week, and more often if the foot has problems. It is more effective using warm water. The foot should be thoroughly picked out before scrubbing. The inside of the hoof and heel area should be scrubbed first, followed by the wall of the foot. It should be allowed to dry before applying hoof dressing or oil.

Hoof brush.

SPONGES

The grooming kit should contain at least two sponges. Medium-sized bath sponges are suitable for cleaning eyes and nostrils, with a separate one for the dock and under the tail. Different colours can help identify them. This should be done daily with the sponge dampened.

Larger sponges are more suitable for bathing and washing off after exercise.

MANE AND TAIL BRUSH

The body brush is the best tool for removing grease from the roots of the mane and tail, but it isn't suitable for de-tangling the hair. Instead, use a specific mane and tail brush. Shorter, thinner manes are much easier to manage than the long, thick manes seen on youngsters or native breeds. The mane and tail brush will effectively remove the tangles without pulling out too much hair. It is easier if the mane is shampooed frequently.

The tail should be separated into small sections to be brushed out. Again this is made easier if the tail is shampooed and sprayed with a tail conditioner.

SWEAT SCRAPER

It is essential to have a sweat scraper to use after the horse has been washed. Its purpose is to remove as much water as possible from the coat. This speeds up drying and prevents the horse from getting a chill. There are several designs of scraper available. It can be used on all areas except the head and lower legs.

SHEDDING BLADE

The shedding blade is a useful item. It looks similar to the sweat scraper, except that one side of the blade has a serrated edge. The tiny teeth are extremely effective in removing loose hair from the coat. It should be used on the neck, body, hindquarters and upper legs. Care should be taken when introducing it, and it

Shedding blade.

MANE AND TAIL COMBS

Mane and tail combs are essential tools for pulling and plaiting. The large comb is useful for combing the mane and separating it in preparation for plaiting. It can also be used to comb the top of the tail. The smaller comb is used when pulling the mane and tail.

The large comb can also be used to trim the feathers using the scissor and comb method.

should not be used on clipped or fine-coated horses. It can also be turned round and used as a sweat scraper.

STABLE RUBBER

The stable rubber is an essential part of the grooming kit. A small cloth, often a tea towel, it is used at the end of a grooming session to give the coat a final polish. It can be used on all areas including the head and legs. It is also used to give the finishing touches before the horse goes into the show ring.

STRAPPING PAD

The strapping pad is not an essential part of the grooming kit. 'Strapping', also referred to as 'banging' or 'wisping', is a traditional grooming practice. The purpose is to help tone and develop the horse's muscles and increase the circulation, which improves the condition of the skin, thereby enhancing the appearance of the coat. The pad can be round or oval shaped and is made of leather filled with saddle stuffing. It has a handle at the back like that of a body brush, making it easier to grip.

The strapping pad must only be used on

Strapping pad.

the large groups of muscles found on the neck and shoulder and on top of the hindquarters. Areas covering the internal organs must be avoided, as should prominent bones. The horse must be confident and relaxed about being handled and groomed before introducing strapping. The muscles must also be sufficiently developed and toned. It is advisable to have the horse held by someone rather than tied up until he is familiar with the procedure. Whenever possible try to strap following exercise when the muscles are warmed up.

Starting on the near side, face the horse with the strapping pad in your right hand. It is very important to be familiar with the groups of muscles that are to be treated. To start, raise the pad and bring it down slowly until contact is made with the muscle. Once the horse is happy with this, speed up the process and press a little harder, developing a rhythm in the strokes. The horse should react by contracting and relaxing the muscle. It should be noticeable that as your arm lifts up, the horse's muscle tenses in anticipation of the action.

Strapping must be introduced gradually, applying no more than six strokes to each area. Increase each time until it is up to twenty to forty minutes per session. Equal time should be spent on each side unless contrary advice has been given by a vet or physiotherapist, perhaps following an injury causing muscle wastage. Strapping also provides a very good work-out for the groom.

HOOF OIL BRUSH

A large brush similar to a paint brush is needed to apply hoof conditioner or oil to the inside and outside of the foot. Some brushes come with a cover to prevent the brush from spreading oil on to other items of the grooming kit; if not, it is advisable to wrap the brush in a cloth when not in use.

Hoof oil brush and cover.

HOOF CONDITIONER

It is advisable to apply hoof dressing or conditioner on a regular basis to maintain or improve the condition of the feet. How often this is done will depend on what is being used and the state the feet are in. Be aware that weather and work conditions often have a negative effect on the feet. Take advice from your farrier on what product to use. The dressing should always be applied to clean dry feet.

HOOF OIL

Hoof oil is applied for cosmetic purposes only when the horse is being shown or competing. It doesn't have the same qualities as hoof dressing, and over-use can be detrimental to the condition of the feet.

TAIL BANDAGE

A tail bandage is not an essential item of the grooming kit but it is advisable to have one, especially for the competition horse. Daily bandaging of the tail for a short period of time will improve the appearance of the tail, especially if it has been pulled. It can be applied

in the morning when the horse is quartered and removed before the horse is worked or put in the field.

PLAITING KIT

A plaiting kit is essential for the competition horse and includes:

- Combs: large and small, used for combing out and separating the mane for plaiting, and pulling the mane and tail.
- Scissors: large and small, used for trimming hair and cutting thread when plaiting.
- Plaiting thread: used for sewing in plaits. Available in different colours to match the mane.
- Plaiting bands: used for securing plaits and laying down the mane. Choose a colour to match the mane.
- Needles: large blunt needles can be used for sewing in the plaits.
- Large hair clips: used to separate the mane during plaiting.
- Quick unpick: used to cut the thread when taking out the plaits.
- Small box or container to store the plaiting kit.
- Plaiting spray.

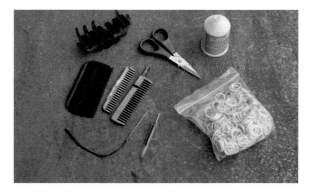

Plaiting kit.

GROOMING KIT BOX

The grooming kit will need to be kept in a box. There are many types of box available in all shapes and sizes to suit different requirements. Fundamentally, regardless of design, the box should keep equipment clean, dry and easy to locate. Boxes that have several compartments are helpful for this. A good sturdy box that is strong enough to stand on often comes in useful when plaiting and pulling the mane.

A well organized grooming box.

PRODUCTS AND USES

Shampoos

There are many different brands of horse shampoo on the market. They range from general everyday shampoos to more specific types for competition. Many manufacturers provide different shampoos to enhance hair colour and help remove tough stains. Other shampoos contain mild antibacterial or antiseptics to help heal or prevent skin problems. It is advisable to try different types to ascertain what suits each horse best. Inexpensive shampoos are ideal for everyday use, with more specific types kept for competition preparation. It is useful to keep an antibacterial wash in stock for treating skin problems when they arise.

Stain removers

Stain removers can be used overnight to dissolve stable stains. Likewise, body whiteners can be applied and left overnight to enhance white legs and markings. Both products can also be used for last-minute touch-ups.

Mane and tail conditioners

Mane and tail conditioners help to keep the hair free of tangles. The tail should be washed and rinsed and conditioner applied before attempting to brush it through. This will prevent the hair from being pulled out. Some products claim to promote hair growth. These can be useful for the mane, especially where hair is lost due to rugs or hoods rubbing the area. The conditioner will, however, leave the mane feeling very silky and therefore should be avoided when intending to plait.

Coat conditioner and gloss

This should be applied to a clean wet coat after bathing or when grooming in preparation for competition. It will give the coat extra shine and help lay the hair down. It does leave the coat feeling very slick, so the saddle area is best avoided as it may cause the saddle to slip.

Coat sparkle

This is often used for the show ring to give extra shine to the coat, mane and tail.

Plaiting spray

Applied to the mane or tail, it permits a better grip on the hair for plaiting. It also helps to hold the plaits in place for longer. Plaiting spray can also be used to touch up the mane during competition if hairs have strayed.

Quarter marking spray

This is sprayed on to quarter markings to enhance them and hold them in place.

Baby oil

Baby oil can be used on an everyday basis when hot clothing. Adding a splash to the water will give extra shine and condition to the skin on a clipped horse. It is often used in competition horses to enhance black areas, such as the eyes, muzzle, under the tail, knees and hocks. Care should be taken in hot, sunny conditions, however, as it may cause sunburn. Baby oil is also effective when used in the tail to give extra shine.

Glistening Oil gloss wipes

These products are used to add finishing touches to the eyes, muzzle, legs and dock area. They are proven to be more effective and safer than baby oil as they contain UV protection to help prevent sunburn.

Make-up skin covers

These products come in various colours and are designed to cover unwanted marks or scars.

Hoof products

Various products can be used on a daily basis to maintain healthy horn. Hoof paints and gloss can be used in competition to enhance the colour of the feet.

4 Routine Grooming

There are several methods of grooming. This chapter looks at the differences between grooming a stabled horse and a horse that is living out at grass.

Horses in their natural environment have their own ways to groom themselves. Rolling allows the horses to relieve its itches and to remove loose hair when the coat is shedding. Horses also like to groom one another. To do this the horses will face each other and use their teeth and lips to scratch along the neck and back. This is also seen when domesticated horses are turned out together or allowed to scratch over the stable door.

REASONS FOR GROOMING

To clean the coat and skin. The horse's skin produces a natural amount of grease. In his natural environment this acts as a barrier against rain, providing protection against cold and wet weather. The stabled horse does not require this, and a build-up of dirt and grease in the coat can cause sores and health problems, especially if the horse gets hot and sweaty during exercise.

To make the horse feel more comfortable. A dirty horse will often become uncomfortable and itchy. This can lead to rubbing of the coat, mane and tail, causing soreness, irritability and poor appearance. The horse will suffer more if the coat is not cleaned after work and rugs are applied on top of dried sweat. This can cause more serious health issues.

To improve health. Daily grooming not only improves the condition of the skin and coat, it also promotes circulation and muscle tone. It also helps to prevent many skin disorders.

To check for injury and ill health. Grooming provides an ideal opportunity to check the horse over thoroughly for cuts, rubs, heat, swelling and pain on palpitation. The earlier a problem is detected, the less likely it is to develop into a more serious condition. It is vital to learn what is normal for your horse so that early signs of a problem can be recognized. This should be done not only with your eyes but also with your hands, which is why it is important never to wear gloves when grooming. The

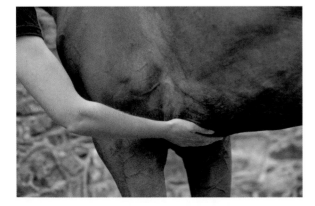

To be able to check for sores, groom without wearing gloves.

A good partnership between horse and groom.

horse may also tell you if he is uncomfortable: for example, if he is usually happy to be groomed but suddenly becomes bad tempered about it, it is usually a sign that he is in pain.

To improve appearance. As well as making the horse feel good, grooming makes him look better. This is essential if the horse is going to take part in competition.

To improve the manners of the horse. As discussed in Chapter 2, a grooming session is also a training session on handling and good manners.

To improve the relationship with the horse. Grooming provides an opportunity for horse and groom to spend time bonding and learning to trust each other. This will benefit the relationship when riding the horse.

GROOMING THE STABLED HORSE

There are various methods of grooming the stabled horse, depending on the time of year and how much coat the horse has. The following describes the procedure for a 'traditional' daily groom.

The horse should be tied up in a safe, suitable area. Choosing where to groom will very much depend on what is available and the time of year, but good lighting is essential, as is a fully equipped grooming kit. The horse's own stable is usually a good place and can be advantageous for horses who have had little handling or can be difficult, as they tend to be more relaxed in their own environment. Some yards have specific grooming boxes or areas. These are well lit and generally have a hose pipe. Often the horses can be cross-tied, making it much easier to work around them. On warm

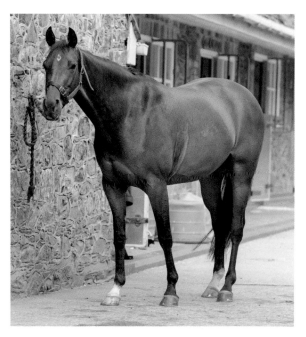

An ideal place to groom on a warm day.

sunny days it is nicer for horse and groom to be outside, but avoid slippery yard surfaces and areas where there is a lot of equipment lying around. Do not allow the horse to be in direct contact with other horses. A quiet area is ideal, as grooming should help to relax the horse, not excite him. Always tie up the horse to a loop of string, or use a quick-release rope. This should make the grooming session a relaxing experience, and avoid accidents for both horse and groom.

Grooming procedure

The old saying 'No foot, no horse' is still relevant today and picking out the horse's feet at least once a day is of the utmost importance. Begin every grooming session,

Picking out the foot correctly.

once the horse is safely tied up, with picking out the feet, always moving the hoof pick away from the heel towards the toe. This makes it easier to avoid making contact with the frog, which is an extremely sensitive structure containing blood vessels and nerve endings. Extra care must be taken with the grooves beside the frog which often run very deep and can cause problems if not cleaned properly. The frog should be gently cleaned using a stiff brush. The cleft of the frog can often harbour problems and special attention should be paid to it.

The foot should not appear too moist or too dry, and should not have an offensive smell. The temperature of all four feet should roughly feel the same; this is best judged by placing the palm of the hand over the wall of each hoof.

If the horse is shod, the condition of the shoes should also be considered. Check for lost, loose or twisted shoes, risen clenches or the hoof becoming overgrown. Most horses will need shoeing every four to six weeks.

It may be necessary for either health or appearance reasons to scrub the feet. The horse will need to be taken out of the stable to do this. It is best done using warm water and a stiff brush. A disinfectant such as Virkon can be added to the water if the feet are showing signs of thrush. Scrub the inside of the hoof first, again paying particular attention to the frog and the heel area. With the foot on the ground, then scrub the wall of the hoof. This will give a better view of the horse's foot and shoe and should be done at least once a week.

The next stage is to groom the neck, mane, body and legs. In cold weather or if the horse is clipped it is not advisable to remove all his rugs: a thorough groom takes around forty minutes, during which time the horse would get very cold. Undo all the straps on the rugs and tie up any that are hanging around the legs, or leave on a duvet or rug that doesn't have straps

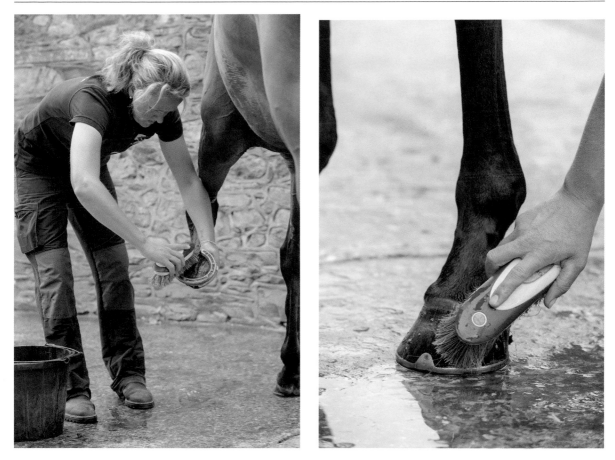

Scrubbing the inside of the foot and the hoof wall.

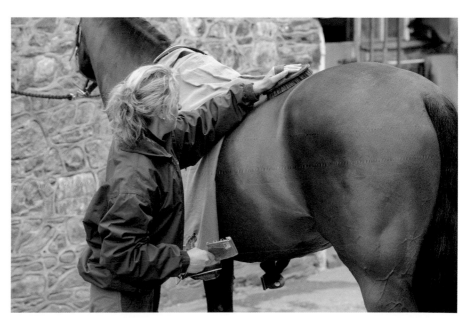

The horse wearing a rug with the straps tied up.

The horse mutual grooms.

The horse showing signs of aggression; he is not enjoying being groomed.

used on most large surface areas, such as the neck, back and hindquarters, but care should be taken when using it under the tummy as some horses are more sensitive here and may kick. It may also be used with care on the forehead and upper leg region. Avoid the lower legs and bony areas. Some horses are more sensitive than others and their reaction should be noted. Signs that a horse can't tolerate it include the ears laid back, tail swishing, attempting to move away, biting or kicking. Most horses tend to enjoy the experience and remain relaxed; some may show signs of wanting to reciprocate. The top lip becomes extended and the horse may try to reach out to the groom, as he would do with another horse during mutual grooming. Care must be taken as this can often lead to the horse using his teeth. This should not be confused with a horse biting.

To use the rubber curry comb, stand at the shoulder facing the tail. The curry comb should be in the hand closest to the horse, so when grooming the off side it should be in the right hand. Start by using the curry comb gently in a circular motion; once the horse is used to it, more pressure can be applied. Work on the area

and is easy to fold in half. The rug can then be folded back when grooming the front end and folded forward when grooming the hind end.

There are several methods of grooming the body depending on how much coat the horse has. If the horse has a full coat the rubber curry comb should be used first. This will bring the grease to the surface of the coat. This is much easier to do if the horse is warm but not sweating, which is why grooming after exercise, when the pores are open, is much more effective. The rubber curry comb can be

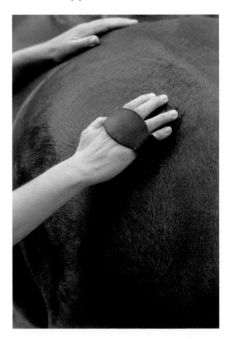

The rubber curry comb is used in a circular motion.

Loose hair and grease is brought to the surface.

Often small cuts, grazes, skin problems, lumps, bumps, heat and swellings are covered by hair and not visible, especially if the coat is heavy. If they are not detected early enough, they can lead to more serious problems.

Checking the legs for injury.

until grease appears on the surface of the coat, then clean the curry comb by banging it on a hard surface. Work from the front of the horse to the back and then repeat on the other side. The grease will be removed from the coat later with the body brush.

The rubber curry comb is also effective for removing loose hair and mud from the coat. It is not necessary to use it on clipped horses.

If the horse has been turned out in the field, the plastic curry comb can also be used to remove dry mud. It can be applied to most areas but care should be taken on more sensitive or ticklish parts. The shedding blade will also remove mud or loose hair but must only be used on large surface areas and is especially effective on the hindquarters. The blade is run across the area in the direction of the hair.

The dandy brush may also be used to remove mud, although finer coated horses are often too sensitive to tolerate it. It must not be used on the legs, face, mane or tail. Starting at the shoulder, brush in the direction of the hair using short, swift strokes. This brush is more frequently used on horses kept at grass.

In this first stage of grooming it is most important to feel the skin and coat with the hand. This must be done without gloves.

After the mud and hair have been removed, the body brush is used on all areas to remove the grease. Stand at the neck, facing the tail, with the body brush in the hand closest to the horse and the metal curry comb in the other hand. The metal curry comb is used to remove the grease from the brush. This should be done as often as necessary and the comb cleaned by banging it on a hard surface.

The mane should be brushed first. This is done by lifting over the mane and grooming the underside. Then split the mane and groom in sections, getting as close to the crest as possible. It will look very untidy at this stage but can be brushed over later. Continue working from the neck, covering the shoulder, chest, foreleg, back, body, belly, hindquarters and hind leg. Repeat on the other side. Long strokes are good for larger areas with smaller strokes for trickier areas. Again frequently check each area with the hand.

Next, part the top of the tail and brush it in sections, getting as close to the dock as possible. The bottom of the tail can easily split and break off so care should be taken. It is better to use the fingers for regular grooming and brush it out only for competition. A mane and tail product can be used to help the tail

The body brush and curry comb are used together.

The curry comb cleans the body brush.

Grooming under the mane to remove grease.

The mane is then brushed down.

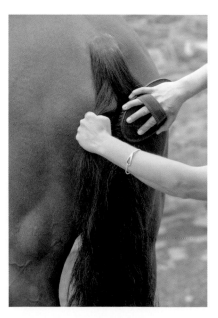

The grease is removed from the top of the tail.

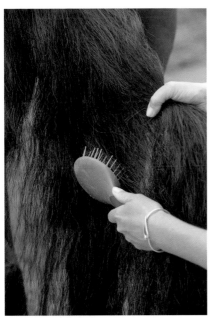

The bottom of the tail can be brushed when well conditioned.

stay tangle free and make it easier to remove bedding. The tail should be washed if there are any signs of rubbing or if it is very greasy.

Lastly, groom the head. It is advisable to untie the horse before doing so. Start at the forehead and brush in the direction of the hair, working down the face, then groom behind the ears and the outer surface of the ears. Raise the head gently and groom under the jaw. The horse sweats a lot in these areas so special attention should be paid to them.

With the horse untied, use a damp sponge to wipe the eyes and nostrils. The horse can then be tied up again. Use a different sponge to clean under the dock. To do this, stand to the side, hold up the tail and gently sponge all areas. It may be necessary to repeat this several times.

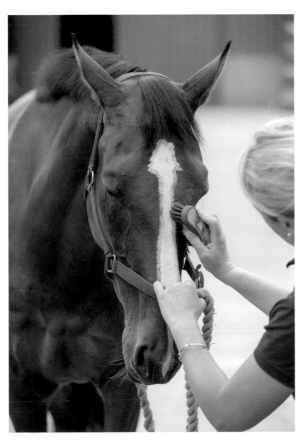

The face brush is used gently on the head.

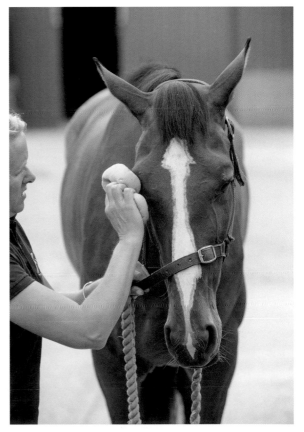

The horse is untied to sponge the eyes.

Sponging the nostrils.

A stable rubber (a dry tea towel or grooming mitt) is then used to give a final polish to the coat, running it over the coat in the direction of the hair. The mane can then be laid over neatly with the body brush and wetted down if necessary with the water brush. Finally a hoof dressing can be applied to the feet. The horse can then be rugged up and untied. The grooming kit should be washed and left ready to use next time.

The grooming mitt is used to give a final polish.

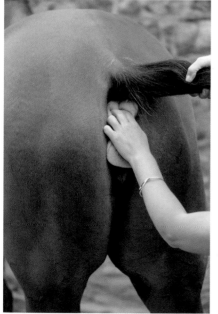

With the handler standing to the side, the tail is lifted to sponge underneath.

Hoof dressing is applied.

A well groomed horse.

GROOMING THE GRASS-KEPT HORSE

The grass-kept horse relies on the natural oils in his coat to protect him from cold and wet weather. For this reason the grooming procedure is different.

The horse living out at grass should be checked daily. (Photo: Shannon Daly)

GROOMING THE GRASS-KEPT HORSE

- Pick out the feet to remove packed mud and stones. Failure to do so could cause lameness. Check the condition of the feet and shoes.
- Remove any thick caked mud from the coat.
- Thoroughly check the horse over for any cuts, swellings or skin problems. Extra attention should be paid to the feet and legs, especially if he is out in wet, muddy conditions.
- Tidy up the horse so he looks presentable for exercise.
- Spend time educating the horse in handling and grooming. This is essential for youngsters.

Grooming procedure

After catching the horse, lead him to a safe place where he can be groomed. This might be the stable yard or a field shelter. Avoid grooming in the field if other loose horses are around. This is a very unsafe practice as horses often relate people to feed time and can get excited or aggressive towards one another. Trying to groom in the middle of this is extremely dangerous. If the horse is living on his own, it may be possible to groom in the field. The horse must never be tied to the gate as he may pull back and lift the gate off its hinges.

Start by picking out the feet and thoroughly checking the condition of the foot and shoes. Horses are much more likely to lose or twist a shoe when out in the field than in the stable.

Horses that live out tend to have heavier coats, making grooming quite hard work. With a plastic or rubber curry comb, remove the mud from the coat. This is not easy if the coat is wet. Next the dandy brush can be used to remove the worst of the dirt from the coat. The body and legs should also be felt over while doing this as skin problems and injuries may not be visible if the coat is very thick. More attention should be paid to the saddle and girth area as the tack is likely to rub if the coat is holding a lot of grease. The neck and hindquarters can be made presentable without removing too much grease.

The mane can be brushed out with the body brush or comb, then the tail brushed out and conditioner applied to prevent it becoming too tangled. The tail should be kept trimmed at the bottom to prevent it becoming too muddy.

Sponge the eyes, nose and dock, and then use a stable rubber to give a final tidy to the coat. Lay the mane and tail with a damp water brush. The feet may require hoof dressing to maintain a healthy condition. The feet of horses living out often suffer more than those of stabled horses. The feet should be scrubbed out before the hoof dressing is applied. In wet muddy conditions a barrier cream can be put on the lower legs to help prevent mud fever and cracked heels.

This procedure should leave the horse looking presentable and healthy without removing too many natural oils from the coat.

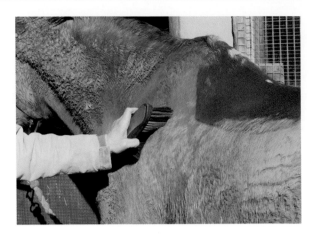

A dandy brush is used on a grass-kept horse. (Photo: Shannon Daly)

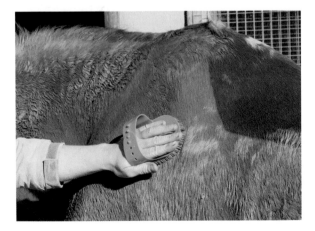

A plastic curry comb being used to remove mud. (Photo: Shannon Daly)

CLEANING THE SHEATH

Cleaning the sheath removes dirt, mud and smegma – a dark waxy substance with an offensive smell. In some cases smegma can be seen outside the sheath on the inside of the upper thigh area. The smell is usually stronger when the horse is warm after exercise. Geldings tend to need their sheath cleaned more often than stallions. It is recommended that it be done every six months, although some vets are of the opinion that the sheath is self-cleaning and should not be washed as it removes friendly bacteria.

Method

You will need warm water, latex gloves, a soft cloth and a sheath cleaning product. The horse should not be tied up if he is unfamiliar or uncomfortable with the procedure. An assistant may be required.

Before attempting to touch the sheath, ensure the horse is happy to be groomed on the belly and inner thigh region. If this is not the case, he will probably need to be restrained or even sedated to allow the sheath to be cleaned.

If the horse appears relaxed and happy, start by using warm water and a cloth inside the opening of the sheath to loosen the smegma. If the horse is not objecting, continue cleaning deeper into the sheath. If the horse is very relaxed, he may drop his penis, making the job much easier. A small pocket of whitish substance can form at the tip of the penis. This is referred to as the bean. Failure to remove this can result in it hardening and restricting the flow of urine. Continue cleaning until the cloth comes out clean. The area should then be rinsed thoroughly. The areas outside the sheath should also be cleaned.

Cleaning the sheath can be an unsafe procedure if the horse's body language is not recognized. If the horse is not happy, ask an assistant to pick up a front leg to help prevent him kicking. This should be done on the same side as the sheath is being cleaned from. If this fails to make a difference, it may be necessary to have the vet sedate the horse. The often makes the job much easier as the horse is more likely to drop his penis. It must be remembered that a sedated horse can still kick, often without warning.

All equipment should be thoroughly disinfected after use.

The sheath should be checked the following morning as occasionally this procedure can cause a minor irritation that will result in the sheath swelling. This usually subsides naturally

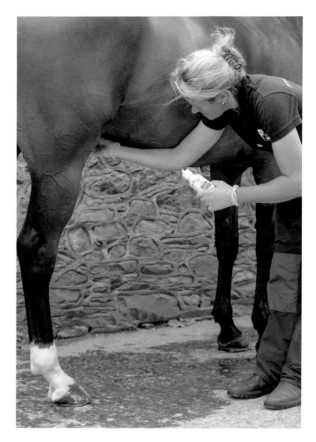

The sheath being cleaned.

within twenty-four hours. It is advisable to give the horse some form of exercise as this should help the swelling go down. If symptoms persist or worsen, seek veterinary advice.

5 Alternative Methods of Grooming

There are other methods of grooming the stabled horse that can be applied in different situations. They are described below.

QUARTERING

Quartering is a method of grooming that is usually carried out in the morning before exercise. The aims are to make a brief inspection of the horse's well-being, to rule out injury and to make him presentable for work. It is much quicker than a thorough groom, taking no more than fifteen minutes. It is traditionally known as quartering, which refers to the folding back of the rugs to access the front end and then folding them forwards to work on the hind quarters.

Procedure

- Tie up the horse in a suitable area for grooming.
- If he is wearing rugs, undo all the fastenings and tie up any hanging straps to prevent them swinging against the horse's legs.
- Start by picking out the feet, making systematic checks of the hooves and shoes.
- Fold back the rugs to expose the neck and saddle region. In cold weather this prevents the horse getting chilled.

The rug folded back to keep the hindquarters warm.

Adjusting the rug for quartering. There are no hanging straps.

- Use the body brush to give a quick brush over all areas, including the legs. As this is done, feel each area with the hand to check for heat, swelling or sensitivity.
- Straighten the rugs and then fold them forward to expose the loins and hindquarters. Brush over these areas, along with the hind legs. The rugs are then replaced.
- Brush out the tail, being careful to remove any bedding.
- Untie the horse to brush the head, then clean the eyes and nostrils with a damp sponge.
- With a separate sponge, clean under the tail.
- Apply a tail bandage and leave it on for a couple of hours or until the horse is worked.
- Adjust the rugs and untie the horse.

Finally the tail bandage is applied.

HOT CLOTHING

Hot clothing is a very effective way of removing grease from a clipped or fine-coated horse. It is less time-consuming than a thorough groom and the horse usually enjoys the experience.

Procedure

Excess water is squeezed out of the cloth.

The cloth is rubbed quite firmly over the coat.

- Fill a small bucket with hot water. Make sure more hot water is readily available in case the first bucketful cools down or becomes dirty.
- Tie up the horse. In warm weather the rugs can be removed, but if it is cold they should be quartered back.
- Add a cap-full of antiseptic Dettol or Hibiscrub to the water to help clean the coat. Alternatively baby oil can be added to give extra shine to the coat. Other products may also be added, such as washes to soothe sore or tired muscles. This is effective after hard training, competition or hunting.
- Rubber gloves may be needed as the water should be quite hot if it is to be effective.
- Ideally hot clothing should be done immediately after work when the horse is warm and the pores are open. This will make removal of grease much easier. If the horse has not been worked, a rubber curry comb can be used to bring the grease to the surface.
- Soak a small towel or cloth in the hot water and tightly squeeze it out to remove all excess water. Starting at the neck, rub the cloth quite firmly in a circular motion over all areas, including the head and legs. Frequently dip the cloth into the water and squeeze it out so that it remains as hot as possible throughout the procedure. This technique will open the pores, remove grease and increase circulation.
- After hot clothing, use the body brush.
- Regular hot clothing will result in a much cleaner, healthier, shiny coat.

WASHING OFF

Washing off is done after exercise when the horse is hot and sweaty. It is not as thorough as process as bathing and usually water is used without products. The advantage of washing off rather than letting the horse dry and then grooming him is that it removes dirt and sweat before the pores close. This will help prevent skin problems. It is also much more time-consuming to groom dried sweat and the horse will often find it uncomfortable.

The horse is offered a drink before washing off after work.

Procedure

- When possible, prepare the washing-off equipment ready for the horse returning from work. Buckets, a sponge, a sweat scraper and suitable rugs are required. Warm water should be used in cold weather.
- Untack the horse and tie him up in a suitable wash-down area.
- In warm weather use a hosepipe to spray off sweaty or muddy areas. In cold weather use warm water and a sponge to clean the saddle and girth area, legs and head.
- Use the sweat scraper to remove excess water from the coat. Rug up if necessary with a suitable cooler or fleece.
- Wash off the legs if necessary, especially between the hind legs.
- Lastly, untie the horse to sponge off the head, paying special attention to where the bridle sits.

- Towel dry the lower legs to reduce the risk of cracked heels.
- Horses often want to roll after work. If the horse is returning to the stable immediately, there is a risk that he may get cast. A horse that is prone to rolling after exercise should be hand walked or put on the horse walker until he is cool and dry.

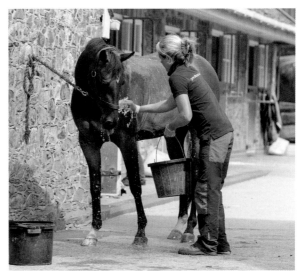

Introduce the water at the shoulder.

Extra attention should be paid to the girth area.

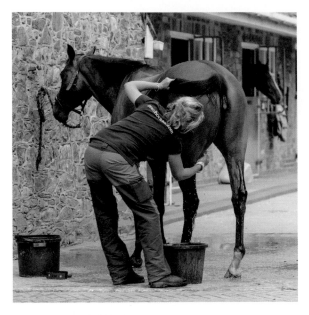

Often the area between the hind legs is forgotten.

The head is towel dried.

Walk the horse until dry if he has a tendency to roll in the stable.

A hosepipe can be used to wash off the horse.

BATHING

Giving the horse a full bath using shampoo and other products is best done during warmer weather, perhaps once a week as part of the grooming routine or in preparation for competition. Avoid bathing in cold weather, especially if the horse has a heavy coat, as it will be difficult to dry the horse and keep him warm.

All bathing equipment should be laid out ready.

EQUIPMENT

Prepare the equipment needed before starting to bath the horse.

- Hose pipe
- Buckets
- Separate sponges for soaping and rinsing
- Shampoo
- Coat and tail products
- Sweat scraper
- Grooming kit
- Towels
- Rugs

Most shampoos do a similar job, and there are numerous products available to suit different colour coats or to treat skin conditions. Grey/white coats often need a specific shampoo to help remove tough stable or grass stains. It is important not to remove too many of the skin's natural oils as this can leave the coat looking dull. Mild baby shampoo is gentle and leaves the coat clean and shiny.

Warm water should be used in cooler weather, or if the coat is particularly dirty, as it is more effective at removing the unwanted grease.

Procedure

- The order and method of bathing will vary depending on the weather conditions. It is much easier in warm weather as the horse is unlikely to get too cold during the process. In cold weather it is essential to keep the horse partially rugged up.
- Tie up the horse in a suitable area with a non-slip floor and close to the water supply.
- Have all equipment close by but ensure that it doesn't get wet.
- If the weather is warm, remove all the rugs. If it is cold, keep on a rug that is easy to fold back and forwards. It is likely to get wet during the process so should not be one that will be worn after bathing.
- Start by picking out the feet and scrubbing the hooves inside and out. This should always be done first as it often splashes dirt on to the legs.
- Next tackle the mane. Again this is done first as the dirty water will run down the neck and body. Wet the mane using either the hosepipe or sponge. When using a hosepipe for the first time, untie the horse to prevent panic. Apply shampoo with your hand, massaging it deeply into the crest where the grease sits. This can be rinsed off immediately or along with the rest of the horse.
- Wet the body and legs using the hosepipe or bucket and sponge. Introduce the hosepipe to the feet first and work up the leg to the shoulder. When the horse is happy, continue up the neck and then gradually work from front to back. Avoid holding the hose over any one area for a period of time as the muscles will quickly become cold. When one side is wet, apply the shampoo. This can be done either by pouring it directly on to a wet sponge or by mixing it with water in a bucket to give a more dilute solution. Most shampoos carry directions for use. The sponge is used in a

circular motion, scrubbing quite vigorously – which most horses enjoy. This can be followed by scrubbing with a soft brush which is more effective at removing stable stains. The lather can be left in the coat while the process is repeated on the other side. Some shampoo products are designed to be left in the coat for a time; if these are used, the tail can also be washed before rinsing the body.

- Rinse off with the hosepipe or fresh water in buckets. Make sure the sponge is soap free, then start at the neck and mane and work back to the hindquarters. The legs can be done either at this stage or later, which is more advisable if extra attention is needed for white socks.
- Once the coat is soap free, use the sweat scraper to remove as much excess water as possible. In warm weather the coat will dry quite quickly if exposed to sunshine. In cold weather a rug should be applied immediately to prevent the horse from chilling.
- Brush the mane over to the correct side of the neck.
- The tail can be washed next. Start by wetting it with the hose or dunking it in a bucket. Apply the shampoo directly to the dock in several areas and work into a good lather. Work down the length of the tail to the ends, then thoroughly rinse and squeeze out the excess water. The tail can then be brushed out. Applying tail conditioner first will make the process easier. Plaiting the tail will help keep it clean and bedding free when preparing for competition. Bandage the tail to help the hair lie correctly as it dries.
- If they have not been done already, wash the legs. Use a soapy sponge or soft brush to remove dirt and stains. Rinse with clean water and towel dry. When preparing for competition, it is advisable to bandage white legs to help keep them clean.

- The head is the last part to be washed and is often the most difficult. Always untie the horse before attempting to wet his face. Never use a hosepipe on the head: if the water accidentally gets into the horse's ears it will cause great upset, often resulting in him becoming head shy. Use a sponge to wet the face and apply a small amount of shampoo. It may help to stand on something if the horse objects and raises his head. Be patient during the process, as it is important to build up trust. Rinse and towel dry.
- Once the coat has dried, use a body brush or stable rubber to finish off. A suitable rug can be put on to keep the horse clean if he is being prepared for competition. Always use clean rugs after bathing and remember to wash the grooming kit.

Always untie the horse when introducing the hosepipe. Start at the feet.

Shampoo is put on the mane using a sponge.

The lather is massaged into the crest.

Continue soaping over the body.

The tail is wetted by placing it in a bucket.

The top of the tail is soaped first …

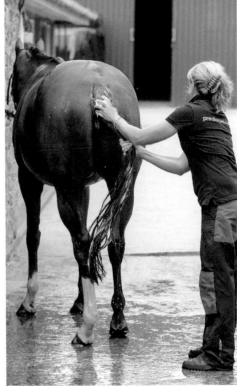

… followed by the bottom of the tail.

Once rinsed, the tail is swung to remove excess water.

Tail conditioner is applied.

The tail can then be combed through.

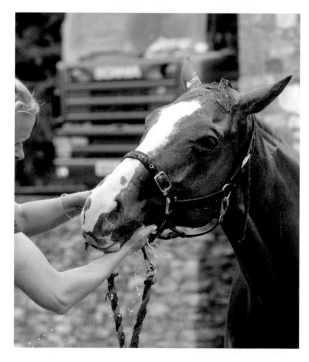

The horse is untied to wash his head. It is important to remember to clean under the jaw.

Care must be taken not to get water in the ears.

The horse is rugged, bandaged and hooded to keep him warm and clean.

Bathing in cold weather

Unless heat lamps are available, bathing in cold weather is best avoided. However, it may be necessary to do so for medical reasons or to clean grey/white horses for competition or hunting. Have all the necessary equipment ready and ensure easy access to warm water. The more quickly the task is carried out, the less likely the horse is to get cold. An extra pair of hands is always helpful.

It is important to cover up as much of the horse as possible during the process. An old duvet is useful for this as it is lightweight and easy to work with. As with quartering, have the

Bathing in cold weather. The rug helps keep the horse warm.

cover folded back and start with the front end. Don't spend a lot of time washing the lower legs as it is often necessary to exercise the horse to warm him up and they will only get dirty again. Wash, rinse and scrape the front half, and then fold the duvet or rugs forward and repeat for the hindquarters. The horse can then be rugged up and walked or gently lunged to warm up and dry. The tail and legs can be done after this. It may be beneficial to apply a hood and stable bandages to help keep the horse warm and dry.

GROOMING MACHINES

An electric grooming machine works like a vacuum cleaner, sucking out loose hair, grease and dust from the coat. As well as giving the horse a thorough groom, it also gives him a gentle massage, opening the pores and increasing circulation. There are advantages and disadvantages to its use.

Advantages

● Reduces the physical effort needed to thoroughly groom the horse.

- Removes loose hair more easily than the curry comb.
- Improves circulation, skin and coat condition.
- Introduces the horse to a machine which makes a noise and feels different on his skin. This may help when introducing clippers.
- Can save time if the machine is permanently set up for use.

Disadvantages

- Very expensive to buy.
- It is not time efficient if the machine has to be set up for use each time.
- Some horses object to the machine and take more time to accept it. This may increase the risk of injury to horse and handler.
- Time is needed to clean the equipment after use.

A grooming machine is probably more suited to larger yards where it can be left set up in a suitable area, such as a clipping box or solarium. Some types are attached to a trolley, which can be quite difficult to move around the horse. Others have a back-pack design which the handler wears and these are more practical. Most come with several brush heads for use on various types of coat. The machine can be used on large surface areas but should not be used on the legs or head.

GROOMING A SICK OR INJURED HORSE

If a horse is confined to the stable due to sickness or injury, it may be necessary to alter his grooming routine. In some cases, for example when the horse is suffering from a virus, he will feel quite poorly and the last thing he wants is a thorough groom. (It may also not be advisable as some conditions are spread

through grooming: this will be discussed in more detail in Chapter 13.) It is, however, still important to carry out regular health checks, pick out the feet and keep his eyes, nose and dock clean.

By contrast, an otherwise healthy horse confined to the stable due to injury may welcome the attention of a good groom as it can help stave off his boredom. Also he may become very itchy due to not having the opportunity to roll in the field. A good going-over with a curry comb or hot clothing will give him some relief. In all cases, read the signs that the horse is showing you. Treat every horse as an individual and assess whether he wants the attention or not: leave him alone if he doesn't want the fuss or spend time with him if he appreciates it.

A sick horse requires only the basic essentials.

Checking a sick horse is essential.

GROOMING AFTER COMPETITION

Grooming after competition or hunting should be left to the minimum. Following a long day of travelling, hard work and reduced food, the horse may feel tired, hungry and possibly sore. On returning to the stable, it is important to remove the rugs so the horse can be checked over. Whenever possible, especially at a competition, try to wash the horse as thoroughly as possible. This is often difficult after hunting and the horse is more likely to arrive home covered in dry mud and sweat. The essential areas to pay attention to are the head, saddle, girth and legs, as these are the sites where problems are likely to occur. Give these areas a wash or brush off, feeling as you go along for heat, swelling, cuts or sensitivity. If he is happy, the horse can be put to bed and given a more thorough groom the next day.

THATCHING

Thatching is a traditional method of drying off a heavy-coated horse in winter and preventing him from getting cold. Put the stable rug on the horse, preferably inside out to prevent it getting wet, and then place underneath it some clean, dry straw to provide a layer between the coat and the rug. The idea is that the straw prevents the hairs from lying flat, which inhibits air flow. Heat is trapped in the straw layer, creating a perfect drying environment and keeping the horse warm. Once the horse is dry, the rug is removed, the straw brushed off and dry rugs put on. This traditional method is rarely used today as modern cooler rugs do the same job.

ROUGHING OFF

Roughing off is the term used to describe the

period of time needed to prepare a fit horse for a holiday in the field. Two to three weeks are needed to prepare the horse mentally and physically for a drastic change in routine. There are several points relating to grooming to consider.

Firstly, the horse will need more natural oils in his coat to protect him from rain and cold. Reduce thorough grooming to a minimum, giving a quick flick-over to check for injury, sponging the eyes, nose and dock, and picking out the feet. Gradually remove rugs to encourage the coat to grow for extra warmth and protection.

Shoes are often removed when horses are turned out. It is important to pay special attention to the condition of the feet when they are unshod, especially in the early stages. For horses turned out in winter, the feathers on the legs offer some protection against mud fever and so these should not be trimmed or clipped. It is a good idea to trim the tail to just below the hocks to prevent it becoming very muddy and tangled. It will also give it a thicker look when the horse returns to work.

Once the horse is roughed off, it is important not to forget the normal regular checks on his health and well-being.

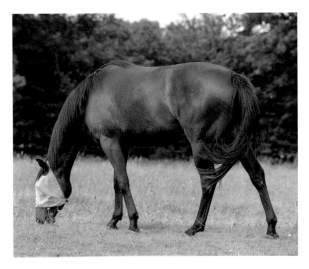

Rugs are removed when roughing off.

6 Trimming

Trimming is done to improve the appearance of the horse. This is of more importance when the horse is being prepared for showing, competing, racing or hunting. It is, however, often beneficial for the horse for comfort and health reasons, for example to keep the mane and tail to a reasonable length. There is a different set of rules when it comes to showing native breeds, which are typically shown in their 'natural' state. Although they are expected to be groomed to a high standard, manes and tails are left long and full. Guidelines on what is required can be obtained from each breed society.

A pulled mane.

This chapter gives a detailed description of methods of trimming, what equipment to use, when it is best to trim and dealing with difficult horses.

MANE PULLING

Pulling the mane is a practice used to shorten and thin the mane. Pulling maintains a natural look, in contrast to the 'chopped' appearance that results from cutting the mane with scissors.

Manes should not be pulled on native breeds

Native breeds are shown in their natural state.

ADVANTAGES OF PULLING THE MANE

● A pulled mane is much easier to manage as it is less likely to get tangled.
● A shorter mane makes it easier to identify and treat problems in that area.
● It improves the appearance of the horse.
● The mane is less likely to get in the way when riding.
● Plaiting the mane is quicker and easier.

intended for showing, nor on horses living out. In winter the mane acts as a barrier against wet and cold weather, and in summer it will help protect against flies.

Procedure

Manes can be pulled using a small metal comb or just fingers. Latex gloves make the hairs easier to grip and offer some protection.

The horse can be tied up if he is familiar with the procedure and relaxed about it. A haynet may provide a distraction. It is advisable to have an extra handler for the first time or if the horse is not happy about it. With a difficult horse, the handler should wear a hard hat and gloves.

Decide beforehand how much mane is to be removed. This will depend on the purpose of pulling. If it is being done simply to manage and improve the appearance, a length of approximately 4 inches leaves it long enough to lie flat on the neck. Thicker manes tend to be more unruly and stick up, so leaving it longer may help the mane to lie flatter. If the mane is going to be plaited, then it must be pulled to help give the right shape for the size of plaits required and to make the job as easy as possible.

Mane pulling is best done immediately after work when the horse is warm and his pores are open. This means that the hair tends to pull out more easily, making it less painful. Do not be tempted to wash the horse as it is impossible to

pull the mane if it gets wet.

If the horse is particularly sensitive to mane pulling, try applying oil of cloves to the crest before starting. This has a mild anaesthetic effect. If the horse still dislikes the idea, it may be necessary to apply a method of restraint, such as a twitch or a chiffney. This enables the job to be done more quickly without fighting the horse. If this fails, it may be necessary to consider having the horse sedated.

Comb method

Start pulling the mane at the centre of the neck; this is usually much thicker and less sensitive than up by the ears or on the withers. Take a small section of mane in one hand, and with the other hand back comb the upper layer towards the crest, leaving a small amount in the

The hair is backcombed, leaving a small amount from the underside.

The hair is wrapped around the comb.

hand. Wrap this tightly around the comb and give a good firm downwards pull to remove the hair from the roots. Repeat the process along the mane until the desired length and thickness are achieved. It may not be possible to do it in one session if the mane has been allowed to get very long and thick. It is better to take more time and keep the horse happy rather than rush and cause him discomfort.

Finger method

If the mane is particularly thin, or the horse is more sensitive, it may be better to remove the hair with the fingers only. Use the comb in the same way to separate the mane, but then, rather than wrapping the hairs around

the comb, simply just give a sharp tug with the fingers. It is important to pull only a small amount of hair at a time. This method may not work with thick, tough manes.

A very small amount of mane should be removed.

Solocomb

The Solocomb is a tool that combines a comb with a cutting blade. The mane is therefore cut not pulled, resulting in a better experience for the sensitive horse. The blade is designed to give a more natural look than cutting with scissors. It is also useful on a very thin mane that requires shortening but not thinning. It is, however, not helpful on a very thick mane that requires plaiting.

Pulling the mane using the fingers.

The Solocomb method.

To use the Solocomb, separate the mane in the same way as for pulling, but then use the blade to cut the hairs to the desired length. There are several types of mane-cutting combs available.

Scissoring

Scissoring is another method of shortening the mane without thinning it, and it doesn't cause the horse any discomfort. Using a scissoring action gives a more natural finish than a blunt cut.

You will need a large pair of sharp scissors. Brush the mane over so it lies flat on the neck. If the mane will not lie flat, try putting it in bunches for a few days before scissoring.

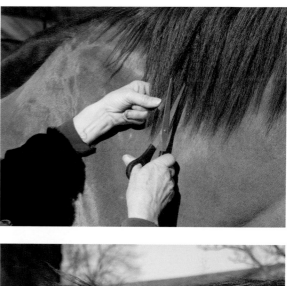

A very long mane may need cutting before pulling.

Decide how short the mane needs to be. If it has grown very long, it is easier to remove some of the length by cutting in the normal way before scissoring. It is advisable to leave it approximately 2 inches longer than the intended finished product. To scissor, cut in an upward direction rather than across the hair. This will leave a more natural look as the ends won't all be the same length. Keep going up and down the mane until the desired length is achieved. If the mane is very thick, use thinning scissors instead of normal scissors.

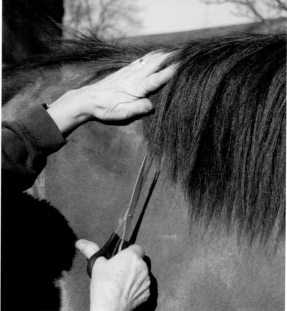

A mane being scissored. (Photo: Shannon Daly)

Cutting

Cutting the mane gives a very blunt and unnatural look. Traditionally this would have been frowned upon but in more recent years it has become quite a popular look, especially on showjumpers where plaiting for competition is seen less and less.

A pair of sharp scissors and a steady hand are required. It is essential that the horse stands as still as possible. Remove the haynet if the horse is eating. Decide on the length required, then start at the top and cut as straight as possible towards the withers. Brush out and straighten up if necessary. The cut mane will end up being quite thick and therefore difficult to plait.

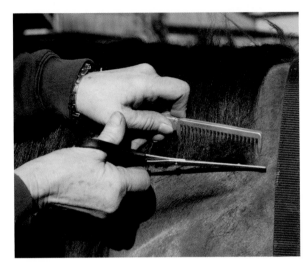

A mane being cut. (Photo: Shannon Daly)

The forelock of native breeds is not pulled.

FORELOCK

The forelock can be pulled, scissored or cut using any of the methods described for the mane. Pulling the forelock into a V-shape gives a more natural look than one that is straight across. Always untie the horse when pulling the forelock and don't stand directly in front of him. If he dislikes the process he may throw his head about and cause an accident.

The following points may help you decide what length to keep the forelock:

- if the horse is living out, a longer forelock will offer protection against flies in summer and rain in wet weather;
- if the forelock is to be plaited, it will be easier to do so if it has been pulled to just above the top of the eye;
- in native breeds the forelock should be left natural, and often reaches halfway down the face;
- consider the appearance of the horse and what length suits his face.

This forelock has been trimmed.

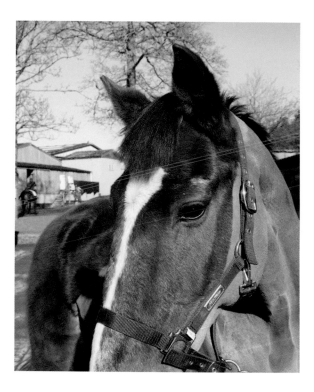

The forelock is pulled into a V-shape. (Photo: Shannon Daly)

HOGGING

Hogging involves removing all the mane with clippers and is most commonly seen on cobs or polo ponies. Cobs in particular are often seen hogged in the show ring. The look tends to suit smaller horses or ponies with a stocky build. It is not advisable to hog the mane of a more thoroughbred type as this will often leave the neck looking poor and weak. Polo ponies are hogged to prevent the mallet getting caught up in the mane.

Before hogging, consider the horse's conformation and lifestyle. A hogged mane will not complement a weak, underdeveloped neck. The mane also offers protection against flies and helps the rain run off the neck. Thus hogging may not be the best option for horses living out without protective neck covers.

A mane may sometimes need to be hogged for treating or preventing health problems. It may also be the best solution for a mane that has been badly neglected, is in poor condition or has become very tangled. This enables new growth of healthier hair.

Procedure

Before hogging, ensure the clippers are in good working order and the blades are sharp. The horse must be familiar and happy with the clippers as he has to accept them around his head and ears. Often a small cordless handset is easier to use.

Wash the mane the day before. A clean mane is much easier to clip than a dirty or greasy one. If the mane is very long, cut it with scissors to approximately 2 inches in length.

Familiarize the horse with the clippers. Start at the withers and work up towards the head, as this will help to build up the horse's confidence. It is easier to clip if the horse drops his head and neck. If he is reluctant to do so, try offering some feed in a bucket. Carry on clipping up the neck until the cut is even. The forelock is usually clipped but can be left on if preferred.

Show horses may be hogged in a way to improve appearance. The mane may be left slightly longer on a section of neck that has a weakness or a dip in the top line, which gives the impression that the horse has more neck than he actually has. An experienced person will be required to achieve this result.

A mane will usually need hogging about once a month to keep it neat. It will take around eight months to grow out a hogged mane and train it to lie down flat. As a hogged mane grows out, it will have a tendency to stand straight up. Hoods or neck covers can help train the hair to lie flat on the correct side.

TRIMMING THE BRIDLE PATH

The bridle path is the name given to the section of mane just behind the ears where the bridle headpiece and headcollar sit. The advantage of a bridle path is that it makes it easier to organize the mane and forelock comfortably under the bridle. This is a huge advantage when putting the bridle on a horse that is head shy. The bridle path should be 1 to 2 inches in length, but certain breeds require it to be longer for the show ring. A smaller bridle path is very discreet and not noticeable when the horse is tacked up. It also helps when plaiting, as it creates a clear division between the forelock and the first plait.

A hogged mane. (Photo: Shannon Daly)

The bridle path can be trimmed to make it easier to put the bridle on.

The clippers are used to hog the mane. (Photo: Shannon Daly)

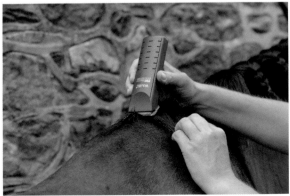

The withers area is trimmed to tidy any stray hairs.

The mane at the withers can also be trimmed to give a smarter appearance when the horse is plaited. Often the mane there is too short or thin to plait. Avoid trimming here if the horse's conformation is weak, as it will enhance the fault.

A longer bridle path is required for certain breeds.

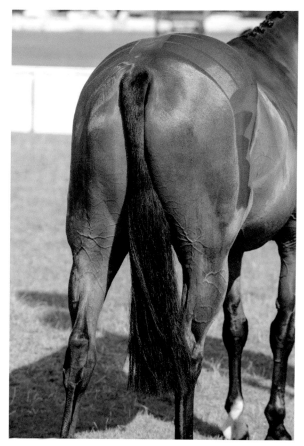

A beautifully pulled tail.

PULLING THE TAIL

The purpose of pulling, trimming or clipping the tail is to enhance the shape of the horse's hindquarters. It is common practice in the showing and competition world as it improves the horse's appearance. It is less time-consuming than plaiting the tail, but it does require time and patience on a regular basis to maintain a high standard.

Procedure

Comb and fingers

Pulling the tail with a comb and fingers is similar to pulling the mane and the same rules apply.

It is easier and more comfortable for the horse if it is done when he is warm after work. The tail must be dry. Some amount of grease will give a better grip on the hair, making it easier to pull out. Avoid washing or applying products to the tail prior to pulling. Use a narrow, small-toothed comb and wear latex or surgical gloves for protection against sores and to give a firmer grip. (It can be difficult to take hold of the very short strands of hair, and a small pair of pliers can be useful for this.)

Personal safety is of utmost importance and must be taken seriously. Standing directly behind a horse who is objecting to having his tail pulled can be very risky. When pulling a tail for the first time, it is advisable to have a handler. Giving the horse a haynet may distract him.

To begin, brush out the tail. Keep in mind what the finished product should look like: the goal is to thin the tail from the top to approximately two-thirds of the way down the dock, with a narrower section level with the point of the buttock, creating a 'waist' in the shape.

Start on one side, taking only two or three hairs from the underside of the dock. Give a sharp downwards tug to pull out the hair. It is usually not necessary to wrap the hairs around the comb. Work for a little while on one side, frequently changing the area to prevent soreness. Repeat on the other side. Standing back to look at the tail will give a better view of how the shape is coming along.

Don't try to do too much in one session as the tail may become sore. Often tiny spots of blood will appear where the hair has been pulled. If the tail becomes too sore, the horse is more likely to want to rub it and it may prove to be more difficult to pull next time.

After a pulling session, the tail should be wetted down and a tail bandage applied for twenty minutes. When the bandage is removed, the hair will be flat and will give a much better impression of how the pulling is progressing.

Sessions should be repeated until the finished look is achieved. This may take up to a week. Keeping on top of a pulled tail requires little bits to be done during each grooming session.

A pulled tail should be bandaged daily for a short period of time to encourage it to lie neatly and to prevent rubbing.

Pulling the tail with the comb.

Using the fingers to pull the tail.

Pulling the tail over the stable door. (Photo: Shannon Daly)

The thinning comb

If the horse is particularly sensitive, objects to his tail being pulled or has a very thick tail, the thinning comb offers a useful alternative. The comb is used in a downward manner, removing the hair from the side of the dock until the desired shape is achieved. Similar to pulling, this gives a very natural look to the tail.

Scissors

The long hair at the side of the dock can be cut with scissors. This doesn't give such a natural look and the hairs tend to stick out rather than lie flat. The scissors should be used in an upward direction. This method doesn't give the best result but can be a safer option on very difficult horses.

Clippers

The clippers are another alternative for horses that cannot tolerate their tail being pulled. Small hand clippers are advisable as large clippers can be more difficult to handle and there is a risk that too much hair may be removed. The result is a very unnatural look and new growth tends to be very spiky and unappealing.

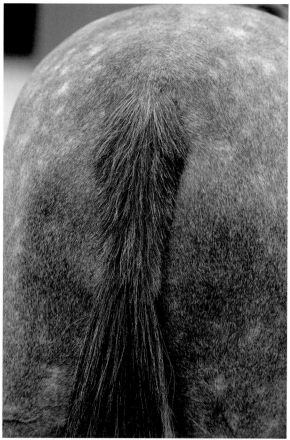

A tail that has been trimmed using clippers.

LENGTH OF THE TAIL

After pulling the tail, address the length. Decide beforehand how long the tail should be. The average length seen on most riding horses is about level with the chestnut, but it may be more practical to have it shorter if the horse regularly works in muddy conditions. Hunters and racehorses are often seen with shorter tails. The current trend for dressage horses and showjumpers is to have the tail longer. This may certainly benefit a dressage horse if it does not have good hind leg conformation. The tails of show horses, of course, must be cut to the correct length for their breed and class. Often native breeds require the tail to be left in its natural state.

A tail that needs cutting at the bottom.

The tail should be clean and thoroughly brushed out, removing all tangles. Run one hand down the length of the tail, stopping at the required length. Cut to length with a large pair of sharp scissors or clippers. Clippers give a much sharper edge and are better for show or competition horses.

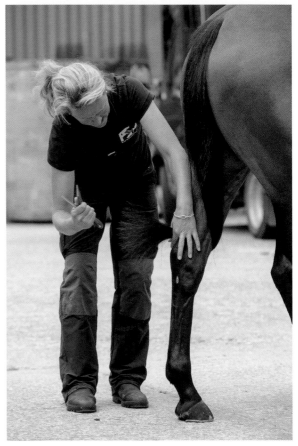

Estimating how much tail to remove.

TRIMMING THE EARS

Trimming the hair inside the ears will improve the appearance of a clipped or fine-coated horse. It should not be done on horses that are living out as the hair offers protection against rain, dust and bugs. If the ears have

TIPS TO AVOID GETTING KICKED WHEN PULLING A TAIL

● Always have someone holding the horse.
● Mild restraint may help such as twisting the skin on the neck or holding up a front leg. In extreme cases a twitch may be used.
● Put the horse in the stable with his tail over the door.
● Do not be in a hurry.
● Take very little hair at a time until the horse is used to it. The skin tends to toughen the more it is done, making the horse more resilient.

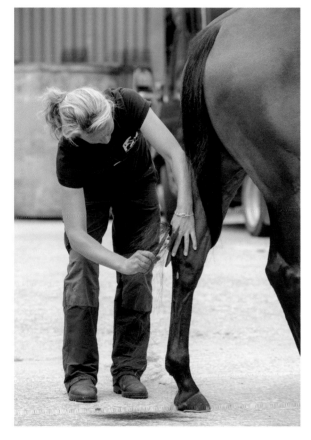

A sharp pair of scissors is required to cut the tail.

A well cut tail.

to be clipped for showing purposes, a mask with ears should be worn in summer to offer protection.

The ears can be trimmed using scissors or clippers. The clippers achieve the best result if the horse will tolerate them. Small hand clippers are quieter and easier to handle. The horse must be happy about having his ears touched and groomed before attempting to trim them.

The inside of the ears can be trimmed if the horse will tolerate it.

Procedure

Always untie the horse and have a handler to hold him if he is unfamiliar with the procedure or is likely to be tricky about it. Close the ear together with one hand, and cut or clip any protruding hair. The hair inside the ears can also be clipped for an even tidier look. The disadvantage of this is that it makes the horse super-sensitive to anything that finds its way into the ears, such as a bug or a rain drop, causing him to shake his head. If this were to happen during competition, such as a dressage test, it would have a dramatic effect on performance.

TRIMMING THE FACE

Trimming the whiskers and jaw line undoubtedly tidies up the face and gives the head a more defined look, which will be an advantage in the show ring. Whether it is acceptable to trim

The whiskers can be trimmed using hand clippers.

the whiskers is a very controversial subject. Many people believe the whiskers play a very important role in aiding the horse to feel and communicate. This, of course, is very important for horses living in the wild but less so for domesticated horses that have food and water available and a safe environment in which to live.

Procedure

The whiskers and jaw line can be trimmed with clippers, scissors or a razor. The clippers are

easy to use and give the best finish. Scissors do not clip as close and it is very easy to catch the horse if he moves, while the razor often takes off some of the skin and can leave the muzzle looking patchy.

Always untie the horse. A head collar with a clip at the side is useful as it allows access to the jaw line without having to remove it altogether. Use the clippers on the jaw line *against* the direction of the hair, removing the cat hairs. The whiskers can then be removed. Some horses may find this quite ticklish and patience is needed. Removing the whiskers can make the horse more sensitive to things touching his nose, resulting in him becoming unsteady in his head when ridden. If this problem is noted after trimming, it may be advisable to let the whiskers grow back as it will be detrimental to his performance.

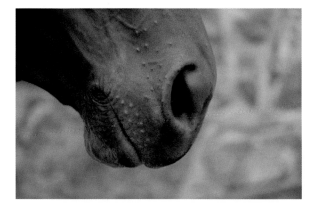

Here the whiskers have been removed.

TRIMMING THE FEATHERS

Feathers are the long hairs that grow on the lower legs. The amount of feather depends very much on the horse's breeding. Finer types such as thoroughbreds have very little, while draught horses and native breeds will grow much more, often from the knee and hock down. Deciding whether or not to trim the feathers will depend on the purpose of the horse and his lifestyle.

The feathers offer protection to the lower legs and heels of horses living out as the rain will run off the hair, helping to keep the skin dryer and less prone to problems. It is therefore advisable

The feathers are left full.

ADVANTAGES OF TRIMMING FEATHERS

- To smarten the appearance of the lower leg for competition or showing.
- Easier to clean and dry.
- Enables problems to be detected more easily. Small cuts or skin conditions can easily go unnoticed if the legs are very hairy and this may lead to infection. Heat and swelling are early signs of problems within a joint, tendon or ligament. Failure to notice any slight changes that may be concealed under the hair may result in a more serious condition.
- Open injuries and skin problems are much more easily and effectively treated on trimmed or clipped legs.

not to trim feathers if the horse is living out in wet conditions. Many native breeds and draught horses are required to be shown in the natural state, so feathers should not be removed if the horse is intended for the show ring.

Procedure

Comb and scissors

The comb and scissor method is the traditional way to trim feathers. A large mane comb and a large sharp pair of scissors are required. The legs must be clean and dry. Run the comb against the hair so that the long hairs protrude through the teeth of the comb, and cut off the excess with the scissors. Repeat until all the long hairs are removed. The result should look very

The feathers are trimmed using the comb and scissor method.

natural and should not show 'steps' where the hair has been cut. The coronet band can also be trimmed if the hair is growing down the hoof.

It is unsafe to kneel down – always crouch.

SAFETY TIPS

- Care must be taken when using clippers or scissors around the legs. Any sudden movement from the horse may result in the sharp blade catching him.
- Always have an assistant if the horse is not completely happy with the procedure.
- Holding up a front leg will help keep the horse still.
- Do not trust even a quiet horse. He may still react to things going on around him.
- Think about personal safety. Avoid being directly in front of the horse when working on the forelegs. A knee in the face can be very painful.
- Always expect the worst when trimming the hind legs.
- Always squat rather than kneel, as this makes it much easier to get out of the way when necessary.

Clipping

Clipping the legs is a much easier method if the horse will allows it. A small cordless hand clipper is ideal for getting into the tricky areas, such as under the fetlock joint. The clippers can be used in two ways. If a grader is attached to the blades, clipping can be done in the usual way, working against the hair. The grader prevents the clip coming too close to the skin and blends in to the rest of the leg. Without a grader, it is better to clip in the direction of the hair, but again it doesn't give the leg such a close clip. The coronet band can also be clipped if necessary.

An assistant holds up the front leg while the hind leg is clipped. It is important that both handlers are on the same side.

7 Clipping

Clipping is a very common practice but it can be quite daunting for someone who has no experience. This chapter advises on when and why to clip, the types of clip and different methods. The aim is to assist in a comfortable, stress-free and safe experience for both horse and groom. It will also help explain preparation and maintenance of the equipment. The help of an experienced clipper is strongly recommended initially.

All healthy horses develop a thicker coat during the winter months. How much hair

Native breeds will grow a heavy coat in winter.

The Arab has a very fine coat.

grows largely depends on the breed of the horse. Thoroughbred and Arab types generally have finer, shorter hair all year round compared to other breeds. British native breeds have evolved to cope with living out in cold, wet weather and therefore grow a much thicker coat. As the horse ages, it is often the case that the coat becomes heavier and does not shed as much in spring. Keeping the horse well rugged and warm may help reduce the growth of the winter coat, meaning a longer interval is possible between clips.

REASONS FOR CLIPPING

Regular heavy sweating without quick drying in cold conditions is likely to be detrimental to the horse's performance. Fluid lost in sweat can lead to dehydration, which is dangerous for the horse and certainly not conducive to well-being. Being hot and sweaty must also feel uncomfortable for the horse, rather like running round in damp clothing.

Clipping enables the horse to work hard without overheating. If a horse with a heavy

Thoroughbred types tend to grow very little coat in winter.

coat is frequently made to sweat hard during the cold winter months, it will inevitably lead to ill-effects. It is very difficult to dry a heavy coat without the horse getting cold. This will lead to discomfort and often loss of condition. The quicker the horse cools and dries after work, the sooner dry rugs can be put on and the horse won't be using valuable energy to keep warm. Wasting energy in this way can quickly contribute to weight loss.

The horse will be more susceptible to skin problems if his coat is thick, especially if regular hard work results in heavy sweating each time.

It is much more difficult to keep the skin and coat of an unclipped horse clean, and thus bacterial and fungal infections are more likely to occur, along with mites. It is also less easy to identify new lumps or bumps immediately, so that injuries or skin damage may go unnoticed until the problem is much more advanced. This will be discussed in more depth in Chapter 13.

Caring and grooming for a clipped horse is much less labour-intensive than for a heavy-coated horse. Thus time and effort can be saved on a daily basis, helping maximize the short days.

Clipping dramatically improves the appearance of the horse during the winter months. This is obviously more important when competing or hunting, but most horses at any level of work will benefit from some of the coat being removed.

It may be necessary to clip during the summer months if the horse is in hard work or the weather is particularly hot. This is often the case for horses competing at higher levels. In eventing and endurance competitions cooling the horse quickly and preventing dehydration are of paramount importance.

A clipped-out horse in full work.

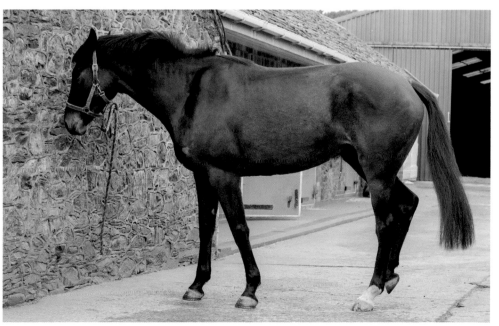

A young horse in light work may not require clipping.

WHEN TO CLIP

Most horses will require their first clip in late September, and it will vary between individuals as to how often it is necessary. Hunters that are working hard and must be smartly turned out may need clipping as often as every two weeks. General riding horses that are not working as hard may only need to be done twice over the winter months. Between October and January the coat tends to grow back very quickly. After this growth slows down, it may be necessary to clip again to retain a smart appearance as the hair that grows now is often of a coarser nature, often referred to as 'cat hairs'.

The last clip is usually done around the end of February. After this the new shorter and finer summer coat will begin to come through, sometimes resulting in a slight change in colour. Growth of the summer coat is stimulated by warmer weather and longer daylight hours. It is not usually necessary to clip during the spring and summer months, but it may be considered if the weather becomes unusually hot or the horse is travelling to a warmer climate.

PREPARATION FOR CLIPPING

Clippers can be expensive, and deciding whether or not to invest in a set will depend very much on how often the horse needs clipping. Other factors include the facilities available, and the presence of experienced people to carry out the procedure safely and teach beginners. There are many freelance grooms who spend the winter months clipping as part of their job. This is often the most cost-effective option for the one-horse owner.

When considering buying a set of clippers, it is advisable to seek advice from a professional regarding the type and make that will be most suitable. Someone who intends to clip no more than four times a year will not require the same heavy-duty clippers as someone clipping three or four horses a day.

It is also advisable to watch a professional groom clip and have an experienced assistant present the first few times. Making mistakes will not only look bad, but may be detrimental to the equipment and an unpleasant experience for the horse.

THE CLIPPING BOX

It is important to clip in an area that is safe and comfortable for both horse and operator. A quiet area away from hustle and bustle is ideal as it will facilitate relaxation, and having another horse close by may help keep the horse calm.

The following points should be considered with regard to the clipping box:

- It must be large enough for the operator to move around the horse easily and safely. It is an advantage if the horse can be cross-tied.
- A high ceiling ensures the horse is less likely to bang his head.
- It must have a non-slip floor, such as rubber matting. If the normal stable is being used, clean bedding should be pushed up to the sides.
- Good lighting is essential.
- There must be a power point close at hand, with a circuit breaker.

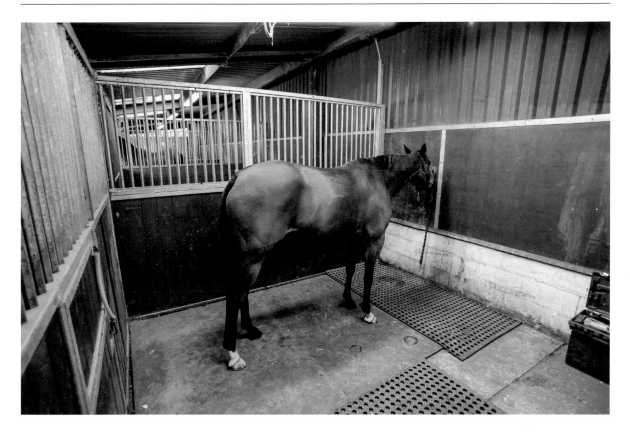

The clipping box is a large area equipped with rubber mats and heat lamps. The horse has company next door which may help him relax.

EQUIPMENT

It is important to have all the clipping equipment ready to use before the horse is prepared. Clipping a horse may take up to three hours, which is a long time to expect a horse to stand patiently. All the equipment should be checked beforehand to make sure it is in good working order. Ensure the blades are sharp enough for the coat and clip intended. It is advisable to have a spare set of blades handy.

The clippers should be set up ready to use with the correct blades fitted. The choice of blade will depend on how thick the coat is and how close the clip needs to be. It is essential to ensure that the tension of the blades is correct. When fitting the blades, tighten the screw to

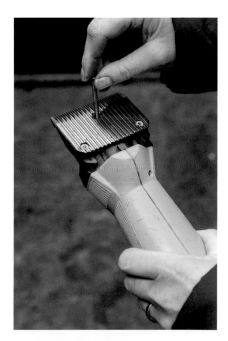

Fitting the blades.

Ensure the tension of the blades is correct.

A circuit breaker must always be used.

the maximum, then turn back one and a half times. Often the screw is marked to help with this. If the blades are too tight, they will heat up much more quickly, and if they are too loose, they will not clip effectively. With experience, it becomes easier to recognize the correct tension by the noise the clippers make.

Checklist for clipping

The following items are essential for clipping:

- An extension lead, long enough to enable safe and comfortable working around the horse. A circuit breaker should always be used.
- Clipper oil.
- A soft brush and a towel to clean the clippers during use.
- A body brush and stable rubber to use on the horse during clipping.
- A sturdy box to stand on for clipping bigger horses.
- String or chalk to help with straight lines.
- A skip, shovel and broom to keep the clipping box clean.

- Suitable rugs for the horse during clipping. If the horse gets cold, it will encourage him to fidget, making clipping him more difficult. Old duvets are ideal as they are warm, easy to fold and do not have straps.
- Suitable clean rugs should be ready to put on after clipping. The horse will require thicker rugs or more layers to compensate for the lost hair. If the neck has been fully clipped out, it is advisable to use a neck cover or blankets. Failing to keep the horse warm enough will result in the coat growing back much more quickly.

PREPARATION OF THE HORSE

It is important that the horse has been well handled and has learned good stable manners. Regular grooming sessions teach the horse to stand quietly and become familiar with different grooming utensils being used on his body, legs and head. The next step is to introduce the noise of the clippers to the horse. If possible, stand the horse in a stable next door to another horse being clipped. This will give him a chance to get used to the noise. When the horse is

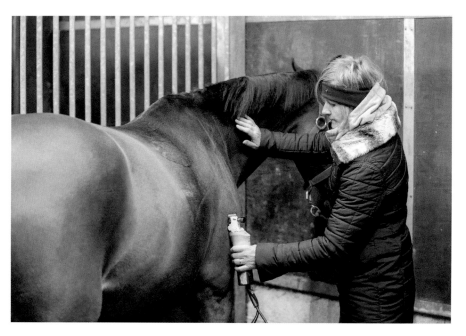

Introduce the clippers at the shoulder. The clippers are not turned on at this stage.

relaxed and looking happy with this, the clippers can be introduced to him.

When clipping for the first time, it is advisable to have the horse held rather than tying him up. If this is not possible, thread the lead rope through the string but don't tie it. This makes it easier to release the horse if he panics. The clippers should not be running when first introduced to the horse. Run the flat part of the blade over the coat in the direction of the hair. As with grooming, the shoulder is a good place to start. If the horse appears happy with this,

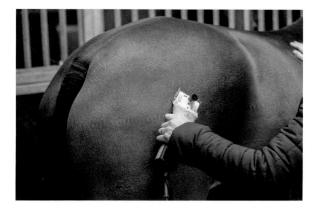

Introduce the clippers to the rest of the body.

continue to introduce the clippers to the neck, body and quarters. Avoid the head and legs at this stage. Always keep the extension lead away from the horse's legs and feet.

The next step is to turn the clippers on. To begin with, do this outside the stable. When the horse looks happy, move into the stable and run the clippers, but still standing back from the horse. Turn the clippers on and off several times, as it is often the sound of the clippers starting up that startles the horse. Once he is relaxed with this, hold the flat part of the blade against the horse's shoulder so he can get used to the vibration of the machine. Nothing can prepare a horse for this and even the quietest may react. If the horse is known to be particularly nervous or ticklish, it may help to place a hand between the horse and the back of the blades to begin with as this reduces the sensation. Continue to move around different areas of the horse. If the horse is not happy with the idea, repeat this step until he is relaxed. This can be quite time-consuming but in the long term is well worth the effort. A horse that has a bad

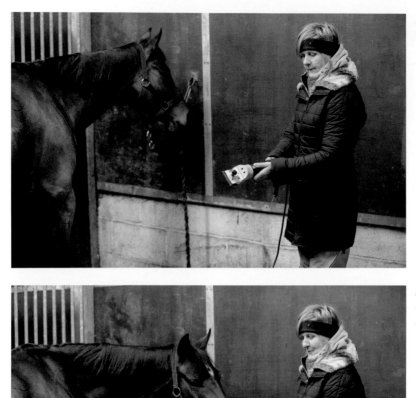

Stand back to turn the clippers on for the first time.

Allow the horse to become accustomed to the noise. This horse is interested but not afraid.

experience the first time will probably never forget it and clipping may be a problem for the rest of his life. This can often result in the vet being needed to sedate the horse each time, which becomes extremely costly.

The horse's coat must be dry and as clean as possible so give the horse a thorough groom before clipping. Mud, grease and dried sweat will cause the blades to tug at the coat, causing discomfort and slowing down the process. Avoid working a heavy-coated horse before clipping as it can take longer to dry than expected. Plaiting the tail

and applying a tail bandage will prevent it getting in the way. A long mane can be put into bunches, making it easier to clip the neck. The horse should be fed as normal as he may fidget more if he is hungry. A gentle stretch beforehand may also help him to settle.

It is debatable whether to provide a hay net or not. It may help to occupy the horse and take his mind off the job, thereby keeping him relaxed. The disadvantage is the horse will be constantly pulling at the net and moving his head and neck. This can make it very difficult to clip the front end, and the whole process may end up taking more time.

PERSONAL CLOTHING

Choosing what to wear for clipping is important. The clipped hair will easily stick to clothing and work its way down collars and sleeves. This soon becomes very uncomfortable. Overalls worn over normal clothes provide good protection and warmth, and are easily washed. Wearing a high collar or scarf will prevent hair getting inside clothing, while large elastic bands worn around the cuffs stop the hairs going up the sleeves. Long hair should always be tied back and a hat worn. If the horse is nervous or tricky to clip, it is advisable to wear a hard hat.

Rubber-soled boots must *always* be worn.

TYPES OF CLIP

Described and illustrated below are the most common types of clip. There may be some variations on how they look.

Full clip

In the full clip, all the coat is removed, including on the head and legs. The only hair that is left on is a small triangle at the top of the tail. This clip is suitable for horses that have heavy coats or are working very hard. It tends to be given to heavier breeds that grow a lot of feather on the legs rather than thoroughbred types. The advantage is that the horse can work longer and harder without sweating so much. Removing mud and sweat after work is much easier and the horse can

---

CHOOSING A SUITABLE CLIP

Choosing the most suitable clip will depend on the following factors:

- How hard the horse is working and how much he sweats.
- How thick the coat is.
- Whether the horse is stabled permanently or living out.
- How long it takes the coat to dry.
- The practicality of changing rugs.
- The horse's temperament. Clipping often makes the horse much fresher and sharper to ride.
- The horse's condition. Clipped horses feel the cold much more and can therefore be much harder to keep weight on.
- The rider's capability. Horses that are ridden by novice riders do not usually work as hard and so will feel the cold much more. A horse who is feeling the cold will have a tendency to be fresh, which may cause problems and become unsafe for a less able or nervous rider.
- How important the appearance of the horse is. Looking smart is more desirable in the case of a hunter or competition horse than it is for a general riding horse.
- Health reasons. It may be necessary to clip the coat if the horse is suffering from skin problems that are difficult to treat when the coat is heavy.
- It is sensible to be more conservative about the choice of clip first time around. More hair can always be taken off if necessary.

be given a full bath without the risk of getting cold as he will dry much more quickly. Injuries and skin problems are much easier to identify, thus reducing the risk of them becoming more serious.

Do not attempt a full clip until the horse is completely happy with the clippers. Clipping the legs is tricky and can be dangerous if done under the wrong circumstances.

There are some disadvantages to the full clip:

● The horse will require thick rugs to keep him warm, including neck covers and sometimes leg bandages.

● Condition will be lost if the horse is allowed to get cold, so turning out time in the field should be restricted on cold, wet and windy days.
● Quarter sheets should be worn during exercise.
● The horse's back under the saddle area may become rubbed, causing him to become sore and sensitive.
● The legs may be more prone to skin problems if regularly subjected to wet muddy conditions. White legs tend to be more susceptible and extra care should be taken.

Full clip. (Diagram: Rozalia Szatanik)

Hunter clip. (Diagram: Rozalia Szatanik)

Hunter clip

The hunter clip is the most common clip given to horses in hard work. The horse is clipped out almost fully, but leaving hair on the back where the saddle sits, either in the shape of a numnah or an oval. This will help prevent the back rubbing and becoming sore. The legs are also left untouched. This offers some protection for the legs in wet, muddy conditions and also reduces the time and risk involved in clipping out the legs. The feathers at the back of the legs can be trimmed to smarten the appearance.

The head can be fully clipped, which will look more professional. If the horse is not happy with the clippers on his face, a half head clip is an alternative and looks quite respectable if done well. The line should follow where the bridle cheekpieces lie and is not that noticeable when the bridle is on.

Blanket clip

The blanket clip is commonly given to horses in light to medium work. It is also suitable for lighter-coated horses, horses in the early stages

Blanket clip. (Diagram: Rozalia Szatanik)

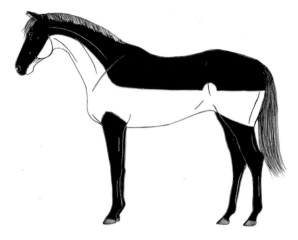

Trace clip. (Diagram: Rozalia Szatanik)

of fittening work and horses spending more time out in the field. The advantage of this clip is that the neck hair is totally removed, which is often where the horse sweats the most. The hair over the back and hindquarters stays on, keeping him warmer and preventing freshness when ridden. The blanket shape can be left quite low or taken higher, removing more hair to suit the workload and depth of coat. The head can be fully clipped or half clipped.

Trace clip

The trace clip is very similar to the blanket clip and would be chosen for the same reasons. Some hair is left on the neck and the head is left unclipped, offering a little more protection.

Chaser clip

The chaser clip is an easier clip to do as the lines are less tricky. It can be taken from the stifle to the wither or from the stifle to the poll leaving some of the neck on. It is a useful clip for horses in medium work or for thoroughbred types with finer coats. It is commonly seen on

Chaser clip. (Diagram: Rozalia Szatanik)

racehorses. It is also a good choice for young horses or ones that are tricky to clip as it does not require too much attention around the hind legs or flanks.

Neck and belly or bib clip

The neck and belly clip removes very little hair so is suitable for horses in light work, horses living out, youngsters and children's ponies.

Neck and belly clip. (Diagram: Rozalia Szatanik)

Start clipping at the shoulder, running the blades against the direction of hair growth.

The hair is removed from the front of the neck, between the front legs and under the belly. The bib clip removes only the hair from the underside of the neck and chest.

CLIPPING PROCEDURE

Before starting to clip, the most important thing is to make sure you have enough time and plenty of patience. Being under pressure to finish will often result in a poor job and stress for both parties. It is better to clip in the morning when the light is good, and it is an advantage to have an assistant.

Once the equipment is set up and the horse is settled, clipping can begin. Before starting, decide on the type of clip and where the lines should be. Inexperienced clippers may find it helpful to allow extra for mistakes and tidying up when both sides are done.

The blades must be frequently cleaned.

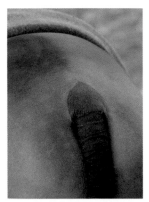

A triangle shape is left at the top of the tail.

The blades must be frequently oiled during the clip.

TIPS FOR SUCCESSFUL CLIPPING

- Draw the clip on the horse with chalk, initially leaving more hair on than intended as this will make it much easier to tidy up.
- Stand away from the horse and turn the clippers on.
- Ensure the blades are fitted correctly and the tension is correct.
- Apply clipper oil to the blades while they are running.
- Turn off the clippers and wipe away any excess oil that has run onto the flat side of the blades. If this gets into the hair, the blades won't run smoothly.
- Run the clippers over the horse's shoulder in the direction of the hair growth. When the horse is relaxed with the noise and feel of the clippers, the hair can be removed.
- Always clip the hair in the opposite direction to the hair growth.
- Try to keep the blades flat against the skin.
- Make long strokes when possible to minimize unwanted lines.
- Go over each stroke a couple of times to ensure no hair is missed.
- Clip lower than the intended line. Corrections can then be made if necessary.
- Remove the bulk of the hair first; once a rough clip is done, turn your attention to the details.
- Leave tricky areas such as the head until last, to avoid the horse becoming upset early on.
- Take extra care where the skin is loose, such as the girth area. Pulling the skin tight will help prevent the horse getting cut.
- Frequently clean and oil the blades.
- Remove hair from the air vents on the handset.
- Stop clipping if the blades feel hot. Rest until they have cooled or change the blades. Ensure when changing the blades that the new ones are the same grade. A fine blade will give a very different result from a coarse blade.
- If the blades are not clipping well, it may be that they are blunt. Continuing with blunt blades will result in pulling the hair, causing discomfort and reduced tolerance. If the blades are sharp, remove them and give them a good clean and oil before continuing.
- Brush the coat frequently to remove the loose hair and check how the clip is coming along.
- Make sure the horse is warm and comfortable.
- Initially do not spend a long time perfecting the lines. Do a rough clip on both sides and then tidy the lines. To help even up the sides, view the horse from behind. If this doesn't help, use a piece of string to measure the length of a line and then match it to the other side.
- It is difficult to clip between the front legs without assistance. If one leg is pulled forward it is much easier to see, and the skin is pulled tight and so is less likely to be cut.
- It is also helpful to have an assistant when clipping the head, unless the horse is very relaxed. Always untie the horse before starting. The head collar may need to be removed and placed around the neck. If the horse is nervous, it will be helpful to use smaller hand clippers. Check that the blades are set to give the same clip as the larger clippers. Start at the side of the head. If the horse is not happy, then it may be advisable to just do half the head until he becomes more confident.
- When the clip is finished, brush the horse off to remove all the loose hair. Check the horse thoroughly under a good light or outside for any missed bits or areas that need tidying up.

Wipe any excess oil from the blade.

It is important to check that the blades do not get too hot during clipping.

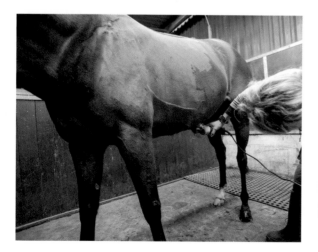

Safety must be paramount when clipping tricky areas.

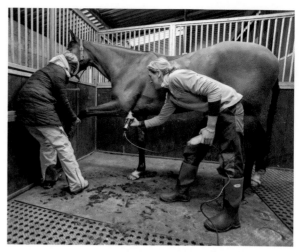

An assistant is used to pull the leg forward.

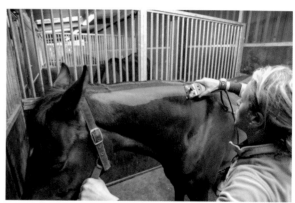

A still horse and a steady hand are required to achieve straight lines.

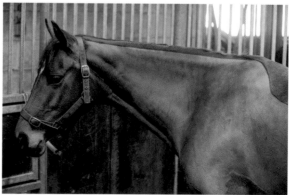

This neat line along the mane requires skill and practice.

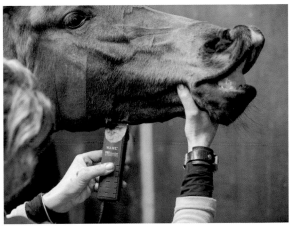

Small clippers are used on the head. The horse is untied and an assistant holds him. Start clipping on the cheek.

Raise the head to clip under the jaw.

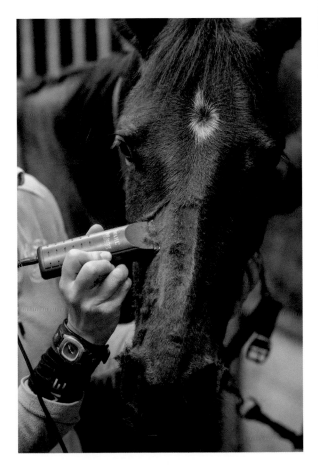

Patience allows the horse to build up confidence.

The horse must be confident and relaxed before any attempt is made to clip the ears.

TIPS FOR CLIPPING DIFFICULT HORSES

Firstly, try to assess why the horse is objecting to the clippers. Listed below are the most common reasons:

- The horse is unfamiliar with the noise of the clippers.
- The horse has not had enough basic handling before the first clip is attempted.
- The horse is not happy in the environment. This is common with younger horses when they are put in a strange box or area for clipping. Putting another horse nearby often helps.
- The horse may have had a previous bad experience. This may include unsympathetic handling, hot blades or being cut.
- A horse with ticklish or sensitive skin may find it difficult to tolerate the feel and vibration of the clippers.

The following procedures will help build the horse's confidence:

The horse should be well handled and confident when being groomed. When the time comes, spend time introducing the noise and feel of the clippers. It is vital to be patient and take your time.

Having an assistant to hold the horse will help to build his confidence and make the situation safer. The handler must always stand on the same side as the person clipping. This enables them to see what is happening at all times and prevents the horse from squashing or treading on the person if he jumps away from the clippers.

Consider some methods of restraint. Holding up a front leg can help prevent the horse kicking out if he is sensitive in some areas. Always pick up the front leg on the same side as the threatening hind leg as horses can quite happily balance on a diagonal pair. Pinching a fold of skin on the neck may distract the horse if he is moving about. A twitch may also be useful if used correctly and safely, but must never be applied for more than twenty minutes at a time and must be removed immediately if the horse is showing signs of distress. Not all horses will tolerate a twitch and it can sometimes cause an adverse reaction.

In some cases the only answer is to have the horse sedated. For a milder effect an oral sedative can be used. This can be obtained from the vet provided the horse has been seen in the previous six months for a health check. If this does not work, the vet will need to give a stronger sedative by intravenous injection. It is important to be aware that a sedated horse can still react quickly and kick. This type of sedative will have a much more dramatic effect and an assistant will be required to help handle the horse as often they can lose their balance. The main practical disadvantage of medical restraint is that it will often cause the horse to sweat, which can make clipping very difficult. It is also costly, involving a vet visit charge plus sedation fee. The sedation tends to wear off after about forty-five minutes, and therefore it is necessary to have an experienced person and good equipment to get the job done in that time.

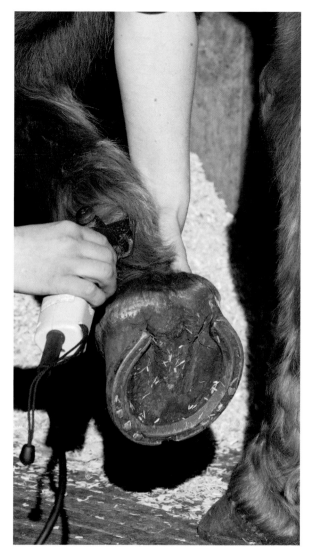

Experience and patience are needed to clip the legs. (Photo: Shannon Daly)

The clippers are used in the direction of hair growth. (Photo: Shannon Daly)

PROCEDURE AFTER CLIPPING

The horse

Brush the clipped areas with the body brush and then give a thorough hot cloth. A small amount of Dettol or vinegar can be added to the water to remove any grease. Any missed areas will now be more obvious. Once satisfied, the horse can be appropriately rugged up.

The clippers

The clippers and blades should be dismantled and thoroughly cleaned before being put away ready for next time. Check the sharpness of the blades: if they feel blunt, they should be sent away for sharpening. Oil them well, wrap them in greaseproof paper and store them in a container to prevent damage. The clipper head should be thoroughly cleaned removing all hair and grease, and also paying close attention to the air vents. At the end of the clipping season it is advisable to send the clippers away for servicing. Make sure the clipper oil is replenished for the next time.

The horse is rugged up appropriately.

The clipper blades are removed and thoroughly cleaned after use.

8 Plaiting

Plaiting the mane and tail is done in order to smarten the appearance of the horse for showing, competing or hunting. For some disciplines it is mandatory, for others it is optional. It is not required for some showing classes of native breeds. Other native classes have their own way of plaiting or decorating the mane rather than the traditional method.

Plaiting is a skill that requires practice to perfect. This chapter explains different ways to plait and how to achieve the best results.

MANES

There are two basic methods to secure the plaits in the mane, one using rubber bands and the other stitching. Once the basic skill of plaiting and securing is mastered, consideration can then be given to the type, size and positioning of each plait so that the overall effect is most complimentary to each horse.

*ABOVE: **Plaiting is a skill that requires practice.***

*LEFT: **A well plaited horse.***

Preparation for plaiting

Practise before a competition to find out how long plaiting will take and if the mane is at an ideal length. Finding out on the morning of a competition that the mane is too short or thick is not helpful and tends to get the day off to a stressful start.

Pull and wash the mane a few days before. A newly washed mane can often be difficult to keep hold of. Never apply mane conditioner as this will make it very slippery.

Have all the necessary equipment ready.

PLAITING KIT

● Large comb
● Scissors
● Needles
● Thread
● Plaiting bands
● Clip to separate the hair
● Water brush
● Plaiting spray
● Box or bag to hold the kit
● Crate or box to stand on

PLAITING

Plait the horse in his own stable or in a quiet area where he can be tied up and stay relaxed. A horse that is fidgeting about makes the job very frustrating and time-consuming.

It may be more practical to plait the night before a competition if there are a number of horses to do or a very early start is necessary. This is perfectly acceptable if the plaits are done well enough and the horse does not have a habit of rubbing his mane. It is advisable to put on a hood afterwards to protect the plaits.

Plaiting with thread

Plaiting with thread gives a much more professional look, makes the plaits more secure and gives more options on the style of plait. It may take longer than plaiting with bands initially but once familiar with the process it can be done quickly.

To begin, brush or comb the mane out and lay it over to the correct side (usually on the right). It is usual to start plaiting at the poll and work down the neck, but if the horse is head shy or difficult in this area it may be better to start at the withers. Using a large comb, divide off a section of hair, about half to three-quarters of the width of the comb. A plaiting band can be placed around the teeth of the comb to use as a guide as it is important that the same spacing is used for each plait. A hair clip can be used to keep the rest of the mane out of the way.

The comb is used to space and divide the mane.

Have the needle and thread ready. For less experienced grooms, it is helpful to knot the end of the thread. Dampen the hair with water or apply plaiting spray. This makes the hairs tacky and much easier to grip. Divide the section of hair into three equal parts and plait down as far as possible, keeping it pulled tight. The plait must be tight to remain intact.

Sew around the bottom of the plait twice, then fold up the end and sew again so the loose hairs are tucked inside. Failing to do this will leave hairs sprouting out when the plait is rolled up. The plait can then be folded or rolled into the neck depending on the desired look.

Fold the plait in half and secure it by sewing into the top of the plait. Then fold it in half again so the plait sits neatly into the neck. Secure it by sewing backwards and forwards in and out of the plait. Alternatively, the thread can be wrapped around the outside of the plait. This will hold a looser plait more securely but may not look as neat. Finish off by cutting the thread at the base of the neck so the end cannot be seen.

The plait can also be rolled from the bottom up to the base of the neck. This often gives a rounder plait, as seen in the show ring. The plait is sewn in the same way.

Repeat the process down the mane. Each plait should be the same size and they should be evenly spaced. There is no set number of plaits, but it is traditional to finish the mane on an odd number, with the forelock making it even.

Experiment with different methods to find the best look for the horse.

The plait must be pulled tight.

The thread is used to sew in the bottom of the plait.

The plait is sewn in by threading the needle back and forth.

Each plait should be the same size and they should be evenly spaced.

Plaiting with bands

The preparation for plaiting is exactly the same, and the mane is divided and plaited down following the system as above.

The bottom of each plait is secured with a plaiting band, folding the end up to hide the hairs as described for sewn plaits. The band should be as tight as possible. The plait is then folded up into the neck and a second band used to secure it in place.

These plaits look neat and are acceptable for hunting and showjumping, but sewn plaits are preferred for showing and dressage. Plaiting bands come in a variety of colours to suit most horses.

This beautifully plaited horse has the traditional uneven number, with the forelock making it even.

PLAITING TO COMPLIMENT THE HORSE

● The size and number of plaits and where they are placed on the neck can help disguise any weakness in conformation or muscle development.
● A short neck may appear longer if lots of small plaits are used.
● A weak neck lacking in top line may appear stronger if the plaits stand up more on the neck.
● Large cresty necks look better if smaller plaits are placed into the neck.
● It is helpful to spend time at shows looking at different horses and how they are plaited.

The band is used to secure the bottom of the plait.

The plait is rolled into the neck.

The band is wrapped tightly.

Bands can look neat but not as professional as thread.

The hooded plaits accentuate the top line.

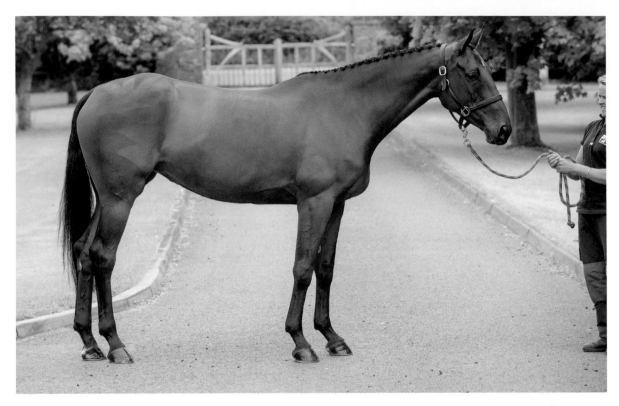

A beautifully plaited and well turned-out horse.

Plaiting the forelock

The forelock can be plaited using either thread or bands. A simple plait can be used, but a French plait looks much smarter. The forelock is prepared in the same way. Starting at the poll, divide the hair into three small sections, and then plait by taking a small amount alternately from each side and continue to the end. This is then sewn in. It takes practice to get this right and requires the horse to stand very still, so assistance may be needed.

All plaits will often need to be tidied and perhaps some finishing touches added before a competition (*see* Chapter 9).

A French plait is used for the forelock.

Laying a mane

The mane can also be plaited in order to train it to lie on the correct side of the neck. It is also useful to practise plaiting. The mane is divided up using approximately a comb's width. It is then plaited down and secured with a band. The plait does not need to be as tight as it would be for competition. The plaits can be left in for a day or two unless the horse is likely to rub.

Alternatively, the mane can be laid over in bunches but this will not be as effective as plaiting. A lycra hood can also be worn to help flatten the mane. It is important to check that the mane is all lying over on the correct side once the hood is on.

Removing plaits

The plaits should be taken out as soon as possible after competition or hunting. Leaving them in longer than necessary may cause the horse to rub the mane and become sore. This is much more likely to happen in warmer weather when midges are a problem.

Removing banded plaits is a straightforward task, but for sewn plaits the thread must be cut. This can be done using a small pair of scissors or a quick-unpick as used for sewing. Be careful to distinguish the thread from the mane. If it is done in a hurry, the mane may easily be cut, leaving short spiky bits that will be difficult to plait next time.

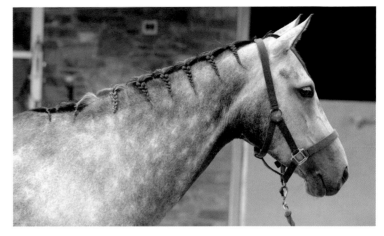

Laying the mane over with plaits.

Bunches can also be used to lay the mane.

The quick-unpick removes the plaits.

TAILS

Plaiting the tail

Plaiting the tail for competition or hunting smartens the tail if it is not pulled. If done well, a plaited tail looks exceptional. Not all breed societies allow the full tail to be plaited for showing. A tail intended for plaiting needs to be full at the top and have good length and thickness. As a plaited tail tends to draw more attention to the hindquarters and conformation of the hind leg, it is not advisable to plait the tail for dressage or showing if the horse has a weakness in this area.

Some horses may carry their tail in an unnatural manner when it is plaited. This may change over time but it is something to be aware of.

Wash the tail thoroughly a day or two before plaiting. It will help if some of the natural oils are in the tail but if it is too dirty the grease will be very obvious. Do not apply tail conditioner as this will make it very slippery and difficult to grip.

Tie the horse up in a quiet area. Plaiting a tail takes time and it can be very frustrating if the horse is constantly moving around. A haynet may help. To begin, thoroughly brush the tail out from top to bottom with a tail brush, separating all the hairs. Wet the top of the tail or apply plaiting spray as this gives a much better grip on the hair.

It may be necessary to stand on a box or a bucket to start the tail off. Have all the equipment easily accessible as it is not possible to let go of the plait once it is started.

Starting at the very top of the dock, take a small piece from each side. Cross the right side over the left, and securing this with a thumb take another equal piece from the left and cross it into the middle. This now gives three sections. Take another piece from the right, and cross it over until it joins the middle

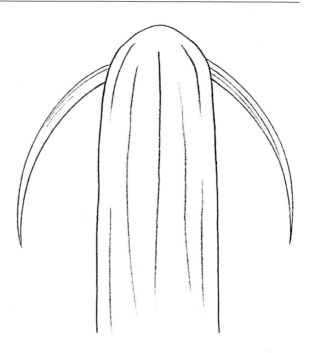

Take a piece of hair from either side. (Diagram: Rozalia Szatanik)

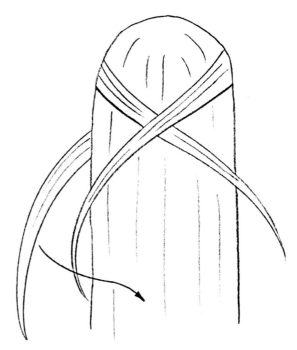

Cross the right over the left. (Diagram: Rozalia Szatanik)

section. Continue down the tail, taking the same amount of hair from opposite sides each time. It is important to keep the plait tight and central.

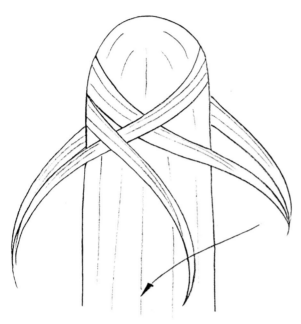

Take a third piece from the left. (Diagram: Rozalia Szatanik)

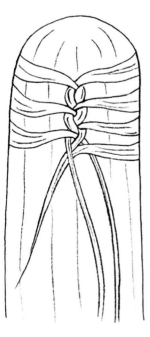

Continue taking a small piece alternately from each side. (Diagram: Rozalia Szatanik)

Continue the plait until three-quarters of the way down the dock. (Diagram: Rozalia Szatanik)

Smoothing the hair down at the side of the tail will help keep the plait tidy. It may be necessary to dampen the tail hairs as the plait progresses.

When the plait has reached three-quarters of the way down the dock, stop taking hair from the sides and continue the plait to the bottom. Secure with a band or thread.

The plait is then folded in half and sewn in at the bottom of the French plait. Continue to sew the loop together to create one thick plait.

The unplaited part of the tail is then brushed out. (If travelling, it is advisable to temporarily plait it to keep it clean.) A tail bandage should then be applied to the plaited part of the tail. Ideally this should stay on until the horse is ready to perform. A second bandage can be applied to cover the rest of the tail for travelling.

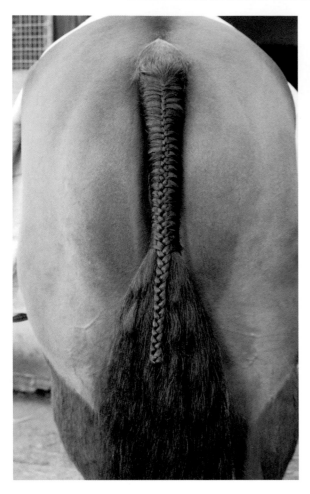

A well plaited tail. (Photo: Shannon Daly)

A tail plaited and taped up for hunting or polo.

When removing the tail bandage, it must be unwrapped and not pulled off as this might disturb the plait.

Final touches to the tail will be discussed in the next chapter.

Plaiting up the tail

Plaiting a tail up is a useful method of preventing the tail from getting muddy in wet conditions, such as hunting or cross-country events. It is seen commonly on polo ponies as it prevents the tail from getting caught up in the mallets. Traditionally tails would have been docked and banged to serve this purpose.

The full tail will need to be plaited using the method described. As it does not show, the plait does not need to be so neat, so larger sections can be taken to save time. When the plait reaches the end of the dock, continue down so that all the tail is in one big plait.

For a pulled tail, the plaiting should start where the pulling stops and be plaited down in the same way. The bottom of the plait is secured using a band or electrical tape.

The tail is then folded onto the dock and then back down again making one neat plait. This is secured in three places with electrical tape.

A neater look can be achieved by folding the plait under the dock and sewing it in place. This may be preferred for the hunting field.

A tail smartly plaited up for hunting.

9 Competition Preparation

Preparing the horse for competition will vary according to the discipline in which the horse is competing, but the fundamental aim is the same: to present the horse groomed and turned out to the highest possible standard. For some disciplines, such as showing, this has a direct influence on the result of the class as the horse is partly judged on how he is turned out. This is not the case in other events, such as showjumping or racing. The standard of turnout does, however, represent the overall picture and demonstrates the

Striving for perfection.

EQUIPMENT CHECKLIST

- Full grooming kit containing various body brushes. Grey horses should have their own brushes to prevent their grey hairs showing up on the darker coats of other horses.
- Trimming equipment
- Water brush
- Hand clippers
- Plaiting kit
- Quarter marking equipment
- Water buckets
- Sponges
- Sweat scraper
- Towels
- Shampoos and products
- Fly spray
- Stool or box to stand on
- Clean bandages
- Clean tail bandages
- Clean rugs

groom's pride in the care and management of the horse.

The following chapters describe how to prepare and turn out a horse to a high standard for a variety of competitions, racing and hunting.

GENERAL PREPARATION

Before going into detail, there are certain aspects of preparation that apply to all disciplines and can be looked at in general.

For any type of competition, it is useful to make a list of all the equipment and products that will be needed before, during and after the event. All products must be free of prohibited substances. This should be stated on the container. It is convenient to have a separate grooming kit to take to competitions, ideally stored in a box that is easy to pack and suitable for travelling.

Clipping

If the horse requires clipping, this should be done about a week before the competition. Often a new clip will show lines and the coat can look dull. A week of hot clothing and grooming will allow time for the skin to produce its natural oils and a shine to return to the coat. Also, if the horse requires sedation for clipping, the withdrawal period on the drugs used must be taken into account.

Trimming

Most trimming can be done a couple of days before, allowing more time for other preparations to be done the day before. Whiskers may be an exception as they grow back quite quickly, so they should be trimmed closer to the event.

CHECKLIST

- Check and feed the horse.
- Complete all yard duties in preparation for return.
- Prepare the horse for competition. Groom, plait and remove stable stains.
- Prepare the horse for travel.
- Finish packing the horsebox.
- Load the horse and make a final check to ensure that all equipment is packed.
- On arrival, lower the ramp and check the horse has travelled well.
- Following a long journey, it is advantageous to unload the horse as soon as possible. Allow him to graze for a few minutes as lowering the head will help to clear the airways.
- Familiarize yourself with the venue.
- Make declarations and entries and collect numbers.
- Ascertain if the competition is running to time.
- Locate rings or arenas and working-in areas.
- Walk courses as necessary.
- Prepare the horse.
- Prepare the rider.
- Allow plenty of working-in time.
- Add any final touches before the competition begins.

The time needed for all these preparations will depend on the number of horses competing, the number of grooms, the temperament of the horses, the time needed to warm up each horse and the distance travelled.

Always leave more time than necessary as more often than not things do not go according to plan. Having some spare time and a chance to relax is more productive for both horse and rider than being stressed and hurried.

Grey horses

Grey horses are more difficult to clean than darker horses. If stains are not washed regularly, they become much harder to remove. This also applies to a white tail.

Making a plan

Make a list of the jobs that can be done the day before and what needs to be done on the day of the competition. This will help with time management. Competing often involves a very early start and it is important not to run late as this is likely to cause stress.

As much preparation as possible should be done the day before. This usually includes bathing or a thorough groom, final trimming and scrubbing the hooves. If the horse is to wear studs, the stud holes will need to be cleaned and plugged. It may also be necessary to plait, but this is better done on the day of competition if possible. Tack and equipment will also need to be cleaned and packed into the horsebox. Equipment needed

Grey horses need bathing on a regular basis. (Photo: Shannon Daly)

for the following morning's preparations should be left out and only packed before departure.

Write down a step-by-step plan of the competition day until a regular routine has been established. This will ensure that nothing is forgotten and enough time is left. The journey time should be over-estimated, allowing for delays in traffic and stops for fuel.

The following chapters will go into more detail on preparing horses for specific disciplines.

10 Eventing, Dressage and Showjumping

EVENTING

Eventing consists of three different phases: dressage, showjumping and cross country. At the lower levels events usually take place over one or two days, but at international level they take place over four days and the horses must participate in two formal vet inspections. The overall image in the dressage phase will look more professional to the judge's eye if the horse is presented well. This may earn an extra mark or two, which could make a big difference to the overall result. At international events a groom's prize is often awarded to the best turned-out horse. This is judged on how well the horse is cared for and turned out during the whole competition.

This chapter describes in detail the care and turnout for eventing, much of which also applies to pure dressage or showjumping.

BEFORE THE EVENT

In the week leading up to the competition all the equipment needed should be checked and any necessary purchases made. The

The dressage phase. (Photo: Shannon Daly)

equipment needed will vary depending on the type and duration of the event. At international events the horse will be required to be turned out on four separate occasions. Sufficient products and plaiting kit should be packed.

Clipping

It is unusual for a horse to need clipping during the eventing season as it runs from spring to autumn. If the horse starts the season in early March he will probably have had his last clip in mid-February and this may need nothing more than a tidy-up. Only if the horse has a tendency to grow a thicker coat, or the weather becomes very hot, will it be necessary to clip again during the summer months. It is more beneficial to the horse if he is able to stay cool during the cross-country phase and will most certainly aid in his recovery. The hunter clip or full clip would be the most practical and presentable, and should be done about a week before the competition.

Trimming

The mane is expected to be plaited for the dressage phase. It is usually also plaited for the showjumping but is optional for the cross country. It should therefore be pulled to a suitable length and trained to lie over neatly. The tail can be pulled or left full to be plaited. The length should be trimmed to complement the horse. The pulled tail should be bandaged for a couple of hours each day so it lies neatly for the competition.

The heels should be trimmed with small clippers or scissors and a comb. This both improves appearance and makes it easier to detect injury.

The face should be trimmed to look more

THE DAY BEFORE THE COMPETITION

- Work the horse in the morning before turning him out in the paddock if this is part of the normal routine.
- If the horse is not being turned out, he can be bathed immediately after work. If the weather does not permit the horse having a bath, hot clothing should be followed by a thorough groom.
- Wash the mane and tail if necessary. Lay the mane over. Brush out the tail and apply conditioner. Apply a tail bandage for a couple of hours.
- Pick out the feet and scrub inside and out.
- Wash white socks and towel dry.
- Clean out stud holes and plug.
- Trim whiskers and bridle path if necessary.
- Plait the mane if time is likely to be short the next morning. The tail must never be plaited the night before as the horse is likely to try to rub it out.
- Rug up accordingly. Hoods and bandages may be applied to keep the horse clean and protect plaits.
- All tack and equipment should be cleaned and packed.
- Prepare the horsebox.

---

defined. Whiskers can be left on or taken off, depending on how sensitive the horse is and personal preference.

ONE DAY EVENTS

Make a preparation schedule, working backwards from the time when the horse needs to be in the dressage arena. Remember to take course walks and travelling time into consideration.

The stud holes are cleaned and plugged. (Photo: Shannon Daly)

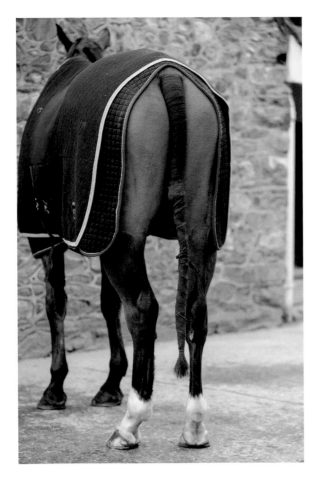

The tail has two bandages for travelling to keep it clean.

Feed the horse. Rugs, hoods and bandages can be removed and he can be checked over to make sure he is in good order.

Plait if this wasn't done the night before, using either thread or bands. The plaits should complement the horse as this will improve his appearance in the dressage arena. A full tail should be plaited. The whole length of the tail can be plaited down for the journey and bandaged to the bottom to help keep it clean.

Give the horse a quick brush over and remove any stable stains. Apply appropriate travel rugs, boots and bandages. Leg protection helps to keep the legs clean as well as preventing injury.

On arrival at the competition, it is advisable to unload and allow the horse to stretch his legs and put his head down to graze. A thick white discharge may run from the nostrils. This is a normal response to travelling. If the horse is not given a chance to allow this to clear, he can often be very irritated when ridden, causing him to snort and cough.

Water should be freely available or offered at regular intervals throughout the day. Once he has had a short walk and graze, he can be put back on the horse box or tied up outside until it is time to get ready for the dressage. It is advisable to remove all food at least fifteen minutes before to ensure his mouth is clean before the bridle is put on. Otherwise he will have a very dirty mouth when ridden.

If weather permits, grooming kits and equipment can be unloaded to make it more accessible.

The dressage phase

This preparation would also apply to a pure dressage horse. It is important to allow sufficient time to prepare for the dressage

A horse beautifully turned out for dressage. (Photo: Shannon Daly)

phase, without rushing and causing stress. When possible, it is easier to work outside; the horse can be tied to the side of the horsebox, or held if an assistant is available. It is important not to allow the horse to graze at this stage. Young horses will stay more relaxed if they can see another horse.

Develop a system which works for the horse and the space available. Always work in a logical order which allows the horse to remain as relaxed as possible and keep warm. If more

than one person is attending the horse, make sure they all know their role and they work as a team. This should be planned ahead so things run smoothly on the day. Once a system for doing things is established, the job will be done smoothly and efficiently.

Care after the dressage

Untack the horse and wash down any sweaty areas. Once dry, brush off the sweat marks. It is important that the horse feels refreshed and looks smart for the next phase. When competing in pure dressage, it is common to ride in more than one class on the same day. The horse should be produced just as smartly for every test.

The horse should then be left to relax until the next phase, suitably rugged and with water available.

GETTING READY

- Remove travel boots or bandages.
- Put in studs if required.
- Remove or quarter back the rugs in cold weather.
- Groom with the body brush. This should not take long as the horse will be clean.
- Check the plaits are intact. Redo and tidy up with hair gel if necessary.
- Remove the tail bandage. It is essential that a plaited tail has the bandage unravelled rather than being pulled off to prevent the plait being disturbed. Brush out the bottom of the tail and apply tail spray or baby oil to give a shine. The plaited tail may need a tidy-up using gel. The tail bandage can then be reapplied and removed just before the horse goes into the arena. This is not advisable if the horse gets upset by the bandage being removed and is likely to kick, or for a young horse that may be very unsettled in the working-in area.
- Sponge the dock and for grey/white horses check that there are no stable stains around the hind legs.
- Apply the quarter markings. In cold weather this should be done after the saddle has gone on, as it is not ideal to put the rug back on over the markings.
- Untie the horse to brush his head and sponge his eyes and nose.
- Put the saddle on. In cold weather keep a rug over the horse at this stage.
- It is not usual to use much make-up for dressage, but a small amount of Glistening Oil applied around the eyes and nostrils is acceptable. Baby oil should be avoided, especially in hot weather, as it can cause the skin to burn.
- Wipe over the body and legs with a stable rubber. Glistening Oil can also be used to highlight black points on the legs.
- Whitening cream or powder can be used to highlight white socks or conceal difficult stains.
- The bridle and boots or bandages can be put on and the horse unloaded if he is not already outside.
- Apply hoof oil. Black oil can be used to highlight black feet. Clear oil looks better on white feet.
- Apply fly spray if necessary.
- It is sometimes possible to do a final touch-up before the horse goes into the arena. If so, a bucket or bag containing a body brush, damp sponge, stable rubber, hoof pick, hoof oil, tail brush and fly repellent should be taken to the working-in area.
- Ideally the final touches can be done about five minutes before the horse goes into the arena. Remove the boots or bandages and the tail bandage. Brush the horse over or wipe with the stable rubber. Wipe around the nose and mouth with a damp sponge. Apply more hoof oil if time permits. Apply more fly repellent if necessary.

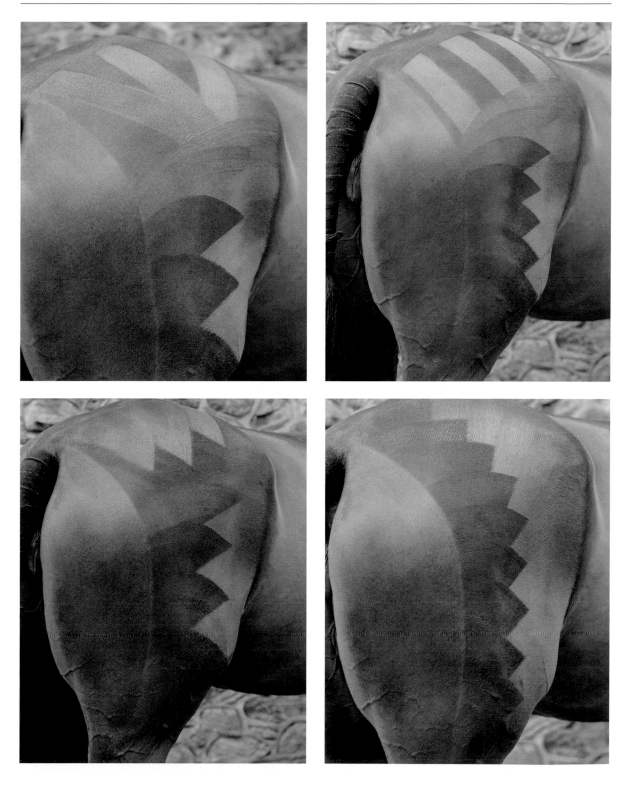

A selection of quarter marks seen on event horses.

The showjumping and cross-country phases

At the higher levels and international events the horse is expected to be turned out to a high standard for these phases and the same routine should be followed as for the dressage preparation. At the lower levels, the horse is still expected to be clean and tidy. The plaits can be removed for the cross-country phase, and this is often the rider's preference.

Care after showjumping

At one day events the cross-country phase often follows shortly after the showjumping. It may not be necessary to untack if the horse is wearing the same equipment, but the girth and noseband should be loosened. Remove the showjumping boots and allow the horse's legs to cool before the cross-country boots are put on. Water should be offered, and if the horse is reluctant to drink his mouth can be rinsed with a wet sponge.

In hot weather the horse should be cooled down as much as possible. This can be done with the tack still on if necessary. Sponge off around the tack and scrape off the excess water. Leather reins should always be towel-dried to prevent them from becoming slippery. The cross-country boots can then be put on and the studs checked and changed if necessary.

Once the horse is tacked up and ready, give a final flick over and brush out the tail. Quarter marks and hoof oil may be reapplied. Grease is optional but should also be put on at this stage, along with more fly spray.

Care after cross-country

The horse is likely to come back from the cross-country phase hot and sweaty; he will require washing to remove sweat and in some cases to get his temperature down to aid his recovery. All the equipment should be ready for the horse's return so this can be done as efficiently as possible. As before, there should be a routine to follow and individuals should know their jobs.

The showjumping phase. (Photo: Shannon Daly)

EQUIPMENT NEEDED

- Filled water buckets: at least two should be available, and more in hot weather.
- Have a separate bucket for drinking water.
- Water containers from which to refill buckets.
- Sponges and sweat scrapers.
- Headcollar and rope.
- Suitable rugs.
- Spanner to remove studs.
- Scissors to remove plaits.

Equipment ready for after the cross-country. (Photo: Shannon Daly)

The horse is likely to finish the cross-country phase tired, hot and blowing hard. Once the rider has dismounted, the girth and noseband should be loosened immediately and the horse walked until he is breathing normally. If the weather is very hot, it is important to cool the horse as quickly as possible. Once the tack and boots are removed, the horse is washed all over and excess water scraped off. Then the horse should be walked around and the whole process repeated until his temperature drops. It is helpful to have three people to do this efficiently. This type of aggressive cooling is usually only necessary at the higher level international events, where there will be vets to monitor the recovery rate and offer advice. Another advantage of aggressive cooling is that it also gives the horse a thorough wash, removing all the sweat from his coat.

In less extreme conditions the horse will cool much more quickly and may not require so much washing. It is, however, advantageous to wash the horse while he is still warm and the pores open, rather than allowing the sweat to dry and having to groom later. Washing also allows time to thoroughly check for injury. There are many products that can be added to the water, such as those containing anti-bacterial agents or herbal substances to help tired muscles recover. Areas that tend to get missed are the head and between the hind legs. Once washed and scraped, a clean rug can be put on if necessary.

The legs should be towel dried and checked over once again. The studs can be removed and the shoes checked. Avoid bandaging until the legs have cooled down. Problems often do not show immediately and therefore may go unnoticed if the bandages are applied too soon.

If a thorough job is done at the competition, very little will need to be done on returning home. Rugs can be changed, legs felt and bandaged if necessary. The horse can then be fed and left to rest. It is advisable to do a late check to ensure all looks well and the horse is comfortable in the rugs he is wearing.

The day after

The horse will most likely have a day off after the competition. A leg stretch or period in the paddock is beneficial. It is not necessary to groom him in the morning, but it is vital that he is thoroughly checked over for any injuries that may have shown up overnight.

Observations on how bright he is, whether he has eaten up, and the state of his bedding are good indicators of general health. After feeding, remove the bandages and rugs. Starting at the neck, run your hands over the body and legs. Special attention should be paid to the back, girth area and legs. The head and corners of the mouth should also be checked.

After picking out the feet, the horse can be trotted up to check soundness. If all looks well, he can be turned out in the field. When he is brought in again, his feet should be picked out

and the worst of the mud removed, his legs checked and rugs changed. This will have given the horse a good day off to recover and his normal routine can be resumed the following day.

THREE DAY EVENTS

At a three day event the dressage, cross-country and showjumping phases happen in that order on consecutive days. There are also two veterinary inspections, often referred to as the trot-up; the first takes place the day before the dressage, and the second one on the morning of the showjumping. The horse must be turned out to the highest possible standard on all of these occasions so will need to be washed and groomed after work each day. As mentioned before, there is commonly a groom's prize that is awarded at the end of the week. This is judged not only on the standard of turnout but also on how the horse has been cared for and presented throughout the whole week. All the horses are stabled together on the site of the competition. The judge will observe the horses

The mouth should be checked for cuts and bruising.

Trotting up for soundness after a competition. (Photo: Shannon Daly)

in the stable, during the competition and also when they are being worked or hand grazed. It is therefore important that the horse doesn't leave the stable without being groomed. For hand grazing he should wear a smart rug and a tail bandage.

For the trot-up the horse should be prepared as for the dressage, but only a bridle is worn. The groom should take a bucket or bag containing the same equipment as for the dressage warm-up to give any final touches before the horse is presented.

As well as being turned out to the highest possible standard for each of the phases, at the higher level events it is common for all horses that are still in the competition to be required to parade before or after the showjumping. Again they must be immaculately turned out for this.

Horse care after a three day event is the same as for the one day event.

DRESSAGE AND SHOWJUMPING

The care and level of presentation required for dressage horses and showjumpers is very similar to that for event horses. For competition the dressage horse is turned out as in the eventing dressage phase, although from time to time plaiting trends or equipment used may differ.

The care and preparation of showjumpers is the same, but the style of turnout differs from eventing. Showjumpers often don't plait, even at the higher levels. Manes tend to be left longer and are cut rather than pulled. Quarter marks are seen less often than on event or dressage horses. Showjumpers should be presented looking clean and polished, with manes and tails washed and brushed out.

Showjumpers are not often seen plaited.

A well turned-out showjumper.

11 Showing

Ridden and in-hand showing classes require the horse or pony to be immaculate in condition and turnout. Presentation in the ring must be of the highest standard and must also adhere to the rules and guidelines set out by the breed society or organization running the show. This information can be obtained when registering a horse or pony, or on the relevant website.

If intending to show it is important that this information is studied closely months ahead. It is also advisable to attend several shows as a spectator to observe the format. If possible, spend some time observing the preparation around the horseboxes or temporary stabling areas. This will give an insight into how best to prepare a horse for a specific class. The collecting ring is also an interesting and educational area in terms of viewing the final touches that are made before the horse enters the ring. It should also be noted what goes on in the ring and what equipment and assistance is permitted.

A native breeds showing class.

Breed societies have their own rules for turnout.

Preparation for showing is not something that can be considered a day, a week or even a month before a show. The rules and guidelines on turnout must be studied well before the season is due to start. Manes and tails will then have time to grow or be pulled to a suitable length, and coats can be worked on to bring them to peak condition. This is especially relevant for horses and ponies that are shown in their natural state.

CLIPPING

Most shows take place during the spring and summer months and therefore horses don't usually require clipping during the show season. They may, however, need to be clipped if working throughout the winter. It

is important to time the last clip so it doesn't interfere with the growth of the summer coat. For this reason clipping should finish by the end of February.

TRIMMING

Before trimming, it is important to know the rules for turnout in the show ring. Information can be obtained from the breed society with which the horse or pony is registered. Most native breeds stipulate that the horse or pony be shown in as natural a state as possible. Some allow discreet trimming, but the mane and tail must remain looking natural and feathers remain on. The jawline may be kept tidy by trimming but the ears and whiskers must not be clipped. Tails are left full and long. If the bottom of the tail needs trimming, this can be done using a blade in a back-combing method referred to as feathering. This will leave the tail looking shorter but not cut. There are slight variations from one society to another, so it is important to make sure the guidelines are read correctly.

Hacks, hunters and show ponies require the horse or pony to be turned out in a more refined manner, and standards have improved dramatically over the years, largely due to the quality of shampoos and products available to enhance the condition and appearance of the horse.

If plaiting, the mane should be pulled to a suitable length. It is very important that the size and shape of the plaits enhance the horse's conformation. As a result, the length and thickness of the mane must be considered.

If the tail is pulled, it should be done in time for it to settle and sufficient bandaging employed to ensure it lies down neatly. The tail should then be maintained on a daily basis rather than allowing it to grow out until the next show. Removing a lot of hair at once increases the risk of rubbing and soreness. A rubbed tail before a show would be a disaster. The tail should be trimmed to a suitable length before the competition. A hunter's tail tends to be slightly shorter than that of the show pony or riding horse.

Small clippers are commonly used and produce the best results for trimming the heels, face, ears and whiskers. This should be done on a weekly basis to keep on top of the job.

GROOMING

Maintaining a healthy skin and coat on a

A shiny coat like this can only be achieved by regular thorough grooming.

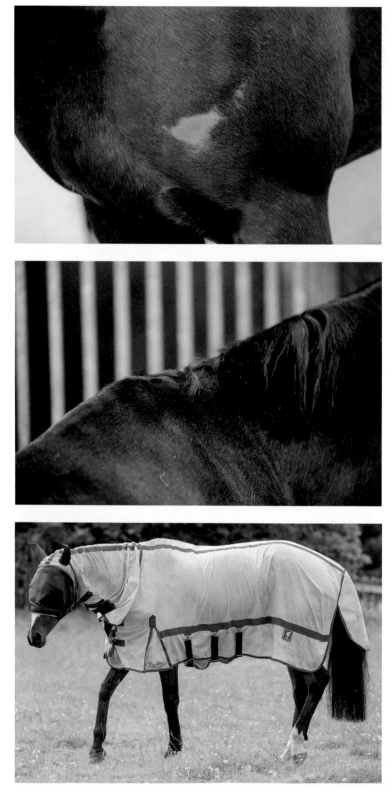

Rugs can cause rubbing at the point of shoulder.

The mane can be rubbed when wearing heavy rugs.

Fly masks and rugs should be worn to prevent sunburn.

daily basis is essential if the horse is going to be in top condition for the show. One bath before a competition will not produce the desired effect. Thorough grooming of full coats should be carried out on a daily basis. This not only keeps the coat clean but also improves the circulation and brings the natural oils into the coat, giving the horse a much healthier-looking natural shine. If the horse has not been clipped, extra grooming will be required in the spring to help shed the winter coat. If this is not done, the hair can take a long time to come out and the coat may not be in top condition in time for the early season shows.

A clipped coat will benefit from hot clothing daily, followed by grooming. Grey/white horses must have stable stains removed on a daily basis, as it is impossible to achieve brilliant whiteness in one wash. Using a stain-removing shampoo and warm water will be more effective.

It is essential that horses are suitably rugged all year round to maintain condition and a healthy looking coat. Keeping the horse warm in winter with rugs, neck covers and bandages will prevent the coat growing too thick. Heavy duty rugs often cause rubbing of the coat and mane, causing hair loss, but lycra rugs, hoods and body wraps can be worn under the rugs to act as an anti-rub layer protecting the mane and neck, the chest area and the point of the shoulder. The rug will also help the coat to lie flat, maintain condition and improve shine. During the summer months it is essential to prevent rubbing of the mane and tail and the sun bleaching the coat. This is more likely to occur if the horse is turned out. Fly rugs and masks should be worn to help prevent this.

A healthy well balanced diet will also have a big impact on the condition of the horse's skin and coat. It is advisable to add a balancer and oil to the feed.

Maintaining the condition of the mane and tail of horses that are left in their natural state is very important. If not given daily attention, the long hair can easily become tangled and difficult to brush out. Regular washing followed by a conditioning product will help prevent brittle hair and breakage. Avoid using a brush or comb as this will pull out the hair and leave the mane and tail looking very thin. Use the fingers to tease out the tangles on a daily basis.

The pulled mane and tail must also be kept clean to avoid rubbing. Horses are more susceptible to this during the summer months when flies and midges are at their worst. Using a citronella-based shampoo is advisable as it has antiseptic, bactericidal and deodorizing properties. It is important to check that any products used do not contain prohibited substances. A fly sheet should be worn at all times. The pulled tail should be bandaged for a couple of hours each day.

During the winter months it is important to keep heavy feathers clean and dry. Failing to do so may lead to mud fever, cracked heels and splitting of the hair. Treating these problems may require the feathers to be trimmed or shaved, and they will take months to grow back to their natural state. The feathers should be washed regularly and thoroughly dried. A barrier cream or powder can be applied daily which will help to waterproof the legs. Pig oil also creates a good barrier and helps prevent mud sticking to them. Mixing it with sulphur also helps protect against lice and mites and keeps the hair healthy. The feathers should be washed, conditioned and a detangler applied before brushing out. The barrier cream or pig oil can then be applied.

In the week leading up to a show, prepare a checklist and make sure all the equipment and products are purchased and ready in good time.

CHECKLIST FOR PREPARATION AND TRAVELLING SHOW KIT

- Assortment of brushes
- Hoof pick
- Sponges
- Stable rubbers and grooming mitt
- Plaiting kit
- Quarter marking comb
- Buckets
- Fly spray
- Shampoos and conditioners
- Detangling spray
- Spray and Shine
- Sparkle Spray
- Quarter marking spray
- Plaiting spray
- Leg and body whitener
- Stain remover
- Cover Magic
- Make-ups
- Glistening Oil
- Highlighter gel
- Wipes
- Hoof paint and gloss
- False tails
- Saddle soap
- Small cordless trimmer
- Travel show box
- Bag or basket to take to the ring
- Small stool to stand on

THE DAY BEFORE THE SHOW

Preparing a horse for showing will require more effort than other disciplines, and the day must be planned in order to accommodate this. As much as possible should be done the day before, as showing usually requires a very early start. It is not unusual for the first class to commence at 8am, which means arriving at the showground for 6am.

Try to have the horses exercised in the morning, leaving the afternoon free to bath, plait (if necessary), clean tack and load the horsebox.

Bathing

Choosing the best shampoo to clean and enhance the coat is important. There are shampoos available for all colours. Choosing a reputable brand such as Supreme Products will save time and produce a top-quality result. Using everyday shampoos will usually result in the wash having to be repeated but the desired effect may still not be achieved.

Dark coats tend to show up grease, while manes and tails can look dirty. Using a show shampoo and conditioner or a high-shine shampoo will strip out the dirt and scurf and restore the natural shine. For best results always use warm water as this will encourage the pores to open for more effective cleaning. The shampoo should be well rubbed in using a sponge or soft brush, and can be left to soak into the skin for ten minutes before thoroughly rinsing.

Grey, palomino and coloured horses will often need several washes to really get the coat clean. As mentioned earlier, daily removal of stable or grass stains is essential to prevent the coat from becoming permanently stained. Use a stain-removing shampoo first as it will be necessary to work quite hard on tough stains. After rinsing, give a second wash, this time using blue shampoo which brightens and whitens the coat. This works on dark coats as well as greys, so is perfect for coloured horses. After rinsing and scraping off the excess water, stand back and look for any blemishes. Spray stain remover on to any stubborn patches and leave it to soak in for five minutes before rinsing.

The mane can be washed at the same time as the body using the same shampoo. In warm weather the tail can be washed before rinsing

A lot of hard work has been put in to produce this brilliantly clean miniature.

A blue shampoo is ideal for coloured horses.

the body. In cold weather it is better to finish the body and apply rugs before starting on the tail. A light-coloured tail will require two washes, first using the stain remover, then the blue shampoo.

After washing and scraping, coat gloss can be applied. This is suitable for all colours and is especially useful on heavier coats as it helps to lay the hair flat. It gives a very natural shine and therefore is acceptable to use on native breeds. Always avoid spraying the saddle area of ridden horses as it leaves the coat feeling very slick and may cause the saddle to slip.

If the mane is to be left natural, it should be sprayed with detangler before being brushed out. The pulled mane should not be sprayed as it will be too slippery and difficult to plait. All tails should be sprayed with detangler and brushed through or teased out with the fingers. Do not spray detangler on the top part of a pulled tail or on a full tail that is to be plaited. The pulled tail should be bandaged for a period of time to ensure the hairs from the dock lie down and don't stick out. If the horse has a tendency to soil his tail it is advisable to put on a tail bag.

White legs and markings

Before washing the legs, ensure the feet are picked out and the hooves have been scrubbed inside and out. If the legs are particularly dirty, wash them first with stain remover before repeating with the blue shampoo. Leg and body whitener can then be applied in the form of a paste or powder. For the best results on trimmed legs mix the powder with water until it is the consistency of yoghurt. Apply to the white socks with a sponge, then put on stable bandages and leave overnight. It can then be brushed out the next morning. The paste can reduce the look of a full feather, therefore the whitener is best applied in powder form when a natural

finish is required. Once the legs are dry, the powder can be rubbed in, leaving a full, shiny, natural appearance.

The feathers are washed using a blue shampoo. (Photo: Supreme Products)

Plaiting

Whenever possible, leave plaiting until the morning of the show. This is more comfortable for the horse and will look much neater. However, this is not always a practical option and plaiting may have to be done the day before.

It is advisable to have experimented with the plaits beforehand to create the best look. Having the correct size, shape and position for each plait can make a huge difference to the overall impression and may help strengthen a weakness in the horse's conformation or

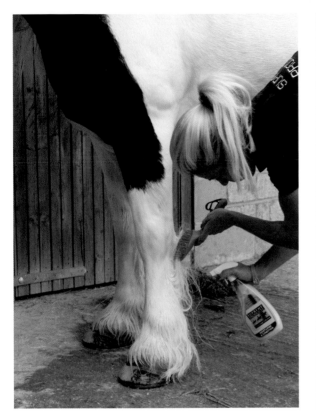

Conditioner is applied and feathers brushed out. (Photo: Supreme Products)

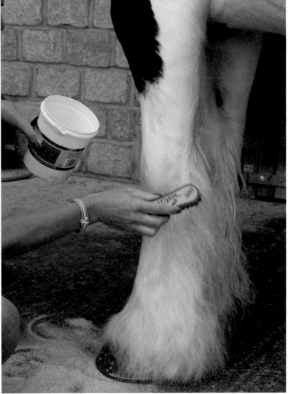

Whitening powder can be used on heavy feathers. (Photo: Supreme Products)

muscle development. Thread should always be used to secure the plaits. Show horses tend to favour the hooded plaits which sit on the crest creating the illusion of more top line. This can be accentuated by placing the plait higher on the neck. It is usual to see an odd number of plaits down the neck, with the forelock making the total even. Using a plaiting spray to help grip the hair will also aid in keeping the plait tight.

Hooves

Once the feet have dried, they can be painted with hoof paint. Always use a water-based paint (as opposed to a varnish) as it allows the foot to breathe and prevents it from drying out. Polish

is available in clear or black to suit the horse's foot colour. It will help keep the hoof shiny and clean and can be touched up the following day.

Rugging up

The horse should be suitably rugged and bandaged for the night. A lycra body wrap under the rugs is ideal as it will protect all areas. If the horse is plaited, it is always advisable to cover the plaits with a neck cover or hood.

SHOW DAY

As with any competition, it is advisable to make a plan for the day. Arriving a couple of hours before a class should allow ample time for preparation. Larger shows may be held over several days and provide temporary stabling. If this is the case, remember to take into account the time needed for unloading and moving horses and equipment to the stabling area.

It may not be necessary to do much to the horse before leaving as he is going to be thoroughly prepared at the show. It may, however, be wise to check a grey horse for

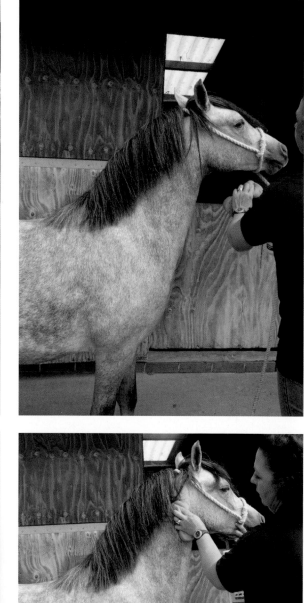

Stain remover can be used to remove last-minute stains. (Photo: Supreme Products)

stable stains and remove them before leaving. Bandages can stay on to prevent the legs getting dirty while travelling. Lycra rugs or body wraps are suitable to wear under travel rugs. The plaits should be protected by a hood or neck cover as it is often easy for the horse to find a rubbing post in the horsebox. Tails must be bandaged and covered to the bottom with a second bandage or tail bag.

On arrival at the show ground familiarize yourself with the layout. There may be a number of rings and working-in areas and it is important to locate the correct one. Collect numbers if necessary. If the weather permits, unload equipment to make it easier to access.

Ridden horses will typically be lunged or ridden to help settle and loosen them before coming back to the horsebox to be prepared for the class. During exercise, try to keep the horse as clean as possible by avoiding muddy areas. The bandages may be left on. After exercise, sponge down any warm areas and allow to dry. While the coat is drying, pick out the feet and scrub the hooves if necessary. The plaits should be checked and any untidy ones redone. Once the coat is dry it should be groomed, making sure to remove any sweat marks. Check for any stains and sponge the eyes, nose and dock.

Start to prepare the horse in plenty of time for the class. It is better to be ready and waiting than to be rushing around and cutting corners. The precise preparation needed will depend on the type of class entered.

The horse is worked before the class to help him settle.

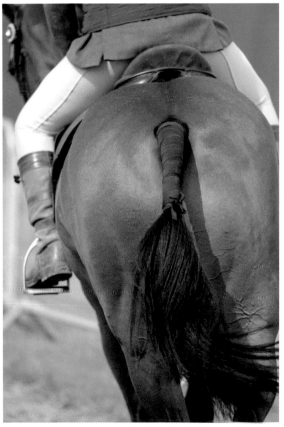

The tail bandage is left on for working in.

TIPS FOR TOP TURNOUT

- Spray the coat with coat gloss, avoiding the saddle area.
- Allow plenty of time to do quarter markings, especially if inexperienced.
- Dampen the hindquarters and spray with coat gloss. This helps to keep the marks in place.
- Use the correct style of marks.
- Finish off by spraying the marks with Quarter Marking Fixing Spray.
- Spray the coat with Sparkle to give an overall finishing touch. This will add extra shine and is effective under artificial lights when competing indoors.
- Horses shown in their natural state should not have quarter markings or Sparkle on the coat.

Finish off by spraying the marks with fixing spray.

Coat gloss is applied on the damp coat.

QUARTER MARKINGS

Quarter markings are applied to the hindquarters or on full coats to enhance the overall appearance. Done professionally, they can highlight strong conformation points or disguise weaker ones. They can be achieved with a brush, comb and stencil.

It is important to choose a design that will complement the horse. Traditionally, hunters have two large stripes. Show ponies and hacks have a checkered pattern. In dressage and eventing a variety of marks may be seen as often a stencil is created for a personal design.

The hair on the quarters is dampened with a water brush or sponge. The large stripes seen on hunters are created by using a body brush with fine short bristles. The hair is brushed in a downward direction producing a mark on the coat. The checkered pattern is created by using a small comb in the same manner. When using a stencil, it should be placed on the hindquarter and the hair showing through the gaps brushed down. Shark's teeth are then added below the above markings. It takes practice to perfect quarter marks and it is advisable to experiment to find the best look for each horse. When satisfied, it is important to stand behind the horse to check that the marks are even. Once finished, Quarter Marking Fixing Spray can be applied, followed by Sparkle Coat Gloss for the final touch. Do not place a rug over the marks.

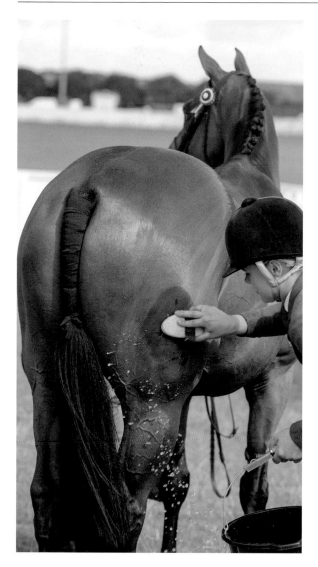

The quarters are wetted with the water brush.

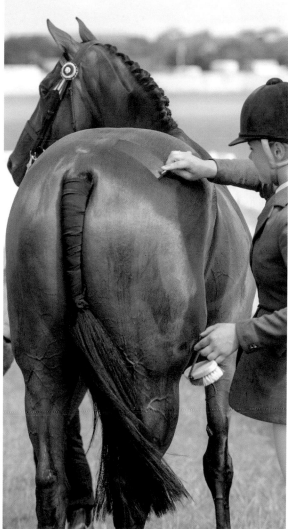

The hunter marks are made using a comb.

Manes and tails

- Stray hairs can be smoothed down using hair gel or Highlighter Gel. This will also give a shine to the plaits.
- Spray the plaits with Shine Spray.
- Natural manes should be brushed out but no products applied unless very discreetly. The shine must look natural not artificial.

- Pulled tails should be brushed out and sprayed with Sparkle to give extra shine. Dampen the top of the tail and reapply the bandage. This can stay on until the last minute.
- Full tails should be brushed out using detangler.
- If the horse has an unnaturally thin tail a false tail can be used. These are available in a wide variety of colours to suit all horses.

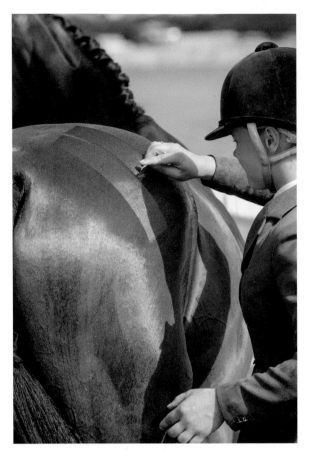

Precision is needed to produce professional quarter marks.

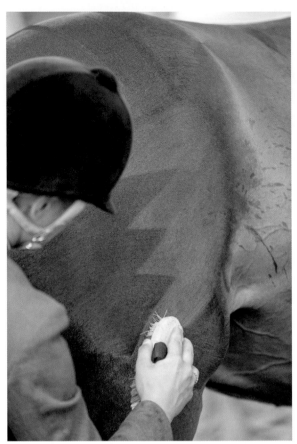

Shark's teeth.

Rugs should not be placed over the quarter marks.

Finally quarter marking fixing spray is used.

Highlighter Gel is used to smooth down the plaits.

Care should be taken when applying dark make-up.

Face

Make-ups can be used to highlight and enhance the features. However, if over-done it looks very unnatural and can work against the horse or pony. Showing in a natural state does not usually permit the use of make-ups.

Baby oil was traditionally used around the eyes, nose and dock and is still seen. The disadvantage of this is that it may cause blistering, especially in hot weather. The show horse can be in the ring for over an hour, standing in the

Make-up is applied around the eyes.

*Overdone eye make-up.
(Photo: Supreme Products)*

sunshine with no shade. Highlighter gel and gloss are now available which are much more effective and contain UV protection.

Make-ups can be applied first. These are available in all colours and should be used sparingly around the eyes and nostrils. Once applied, stand back and assess the appearance; if it looks over-done, remove a little to tone it down. Dark make-ups can be quite messy and care should be taken not to stain competition clothing. If this proves challenging, it can be applied the day before and allowed to soak in. Highlighter can then be applied over the Make-Up and blended across the face.

White markings on the face can be highlighted using whitening cream. This will give the face more definition.

Legs

It is advisable to leave bandages on for working-in, especially in wet conditions. When ready, remove the bandages and brush out the legs to remove any excess body whitener. Apply chalk for the finishing touch.

Black legs should be brushed over and wiped to remove dirt and dust. The knees and hocks can be sprayed with Black Supreme Cover Magic which will accentuate shape and give more definition. Allow to dry and apply Glistening Oil to add shine. Cover Magic can also be used to cover any blemishes on the legs, body or head and is available in different colours.

Full-feathered legs should be thoroughly brushed out and left to look natural.

Hooves

Feet should be picked out and any mud or dirt removed from the hoof wall. Apply Hoof Paint

A final coat of hoof paint is applied.

Always stand back and observe the horse.

if not already done. A hoof gloss can then be applied on top to add shine.

Tacking up

Now the horse is ready to be tacked up, or an in-hand bridle put on. Once the tack is on, always stand back to view the horse from front, both sides and rear. Make any last-minute adjustments if necessary.

Showing is a discipline that cannot be done alone. An assistant is needed to help with the finishing touches after working-in. Some classes also require the saddle to be removed after the ridden section in order for the judge to assess the conformation of the horse. The assistant will enter the ring, the saddle is removed and the horse can be smartened up for the next phase.

After the class the horse can return to the horsebox or stables. In some cases he may be required to go back into the ring for the championship. If so, offer the horse some water and give him a chance to relax until the smartening-up process begins again.

Once the horse has finished, the tack can be taken off and the horse washed if necessary. Plaits should be removed. Food and water can be offered.

EQUIPMENT TO TAKE TO THE COLLECTING RING

- Body brush
- Stable rubber
- Coat spray
- Sparkle
- Fly spray
- Hoof brush and polish

- Chalk
- Quarter marking comb
- Wipes
- Saddle soap
- Bottle of water

A show hunter class. (Photo: Shannon Daly)

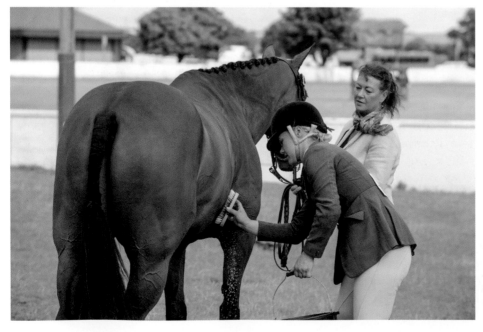

After the class the saddle is removed and sweat marks washed off.

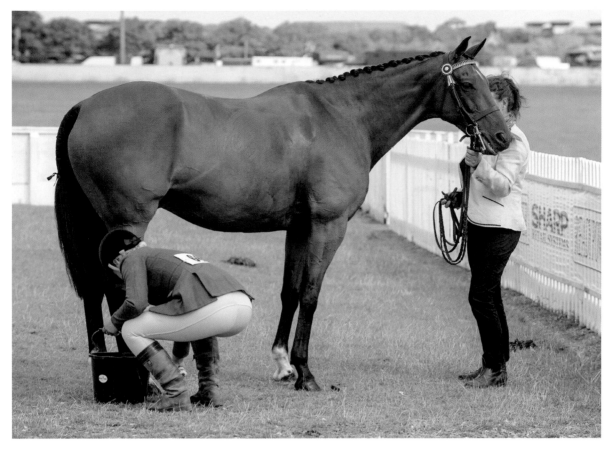

The horse must be turned out smartly for the championship.

AFTER THE SHOW

Although showing is not the most strenuous activity when compared to racing or eventing, it is still tiring for the horse. It is often a very long day and the horse may have travelled a considerable distance. His normal routine has also been disrupted, which can sometimes cause problems.

The horse should be monitored accordingly on his return home. After unloading, he will probably appreciate the rugs being removed and being given the chance to have a roll.

The next day he should be thoroughly checked over. There are less likely to be leg problems but his overall condition should be considered. A long journey and the stress of the show can often cause dehydration and weight loss. Any products that were not removed the day before should be washed or brushed off before giving him a well-deserved day off.

It is advisable to take stock of shampoos and other products and replenish supplies if necessary ready for the next show.

12 Hunting and Racing

THE HUNTER

Although hunting is not competitive, it is expected that all members of the field present themselves and their horses smartly. Hunting dates back as far as the sixteenth century, and was traditionally a sport for the upper class. Gentlemen wore long tail coats and top hats, while ladies rode side-saddle. Although some people may still view hunting as an aristocratic sport, anyone is welcome to subscribe to a hunt or have odd days, referred to as visiting. Children are welcomed and very much encouraged through the Pony Club. Hunting etiquette has remained important, as has the standard of turnout of horse and rider. Occasionally men are still seen wearing a traditional tail coat and ladies riding side-saddle.

Clipping

Hunting requires a horse to be fit and therefore in medium to hard work. The hunting season takes place from November to March, so hunters will require clipping. This will enable

Traditionally men wore top hat and tails.

Ladies hunted side-saddle.

them to cope more readily with the workload and they will be easier to clean after hunting. The traditional hunter clip is discussed in Chapter 7. This is the most common clip seen on hunters as it allows for easier preparation and aftercare. Younger horses that are not doing a hard day's hunting may require only a chaser or trace clip.

Autumn hunting takes place from September to November. This is much slower-paced than hunting proper and often there is no need for the horses to be clipped, or a trace or chaser clip may be appropriate. It is less formal than hunting but still requires the horses to arrive groomed and clean. Plaiting is not expected.

The full clip should be given about a week before the opening meet. This will give the coat time to settle down. Up to January the coat will often grow back very quickly and it may be necessary to clip as often as every ten days.

Trimming

The mane should be pulled to a suitable length for plaiting. Hogging is also acceptable for cobs. Tails can be pulled or left full for plaiting. The

---

PREPARATION THE DAY BEFORE

- Try to work the horse as early as possible, so he can be turned out in the field if this is part of his routine. Bring him in early enough to allow preparation in daylight hours and before the temperature drops for the evening.
- Clipped horses should have a hot cloth followed by a thorough groom. Non clipped horses should be curry combed followed by a thorough groom. Manes and tails should be washed if necessary. A newly washed mane can be more difficult to plait, so washing can be done a few days earlier.
- Trim any areas needing attention.
- Wash white socks.
- Scrub the feet inside and out.
- Rug up suitably for the night. Neck covers and hoods can be used to help keep grey horses clean.
- All tack and equipment must be cleaned.

A child smartly turned out for hunting. (Photo: Shannon Daly)

bottom of the tail should be trimmed an inch or two below the hock to prevent it getting too muddy.

Legs may be clipped out. If not, feathers should be trimmed, although native breeds may keep their feathers. In this case extra care should be taken after hunting to check the legs for injury or thorns.

Heads may also be clipped out. If not, the beard should be trimmed with scissors. Whiskers can be left on or taken off.

HUNTING MORNING

Provided you are hunting with a local pack, the journey to the meet will generally not take more than an hour. Most packs meet around 10.45am. Aim to arrive about half an hour beforehand, giving ample time to get on and hack the short distance to the meet.

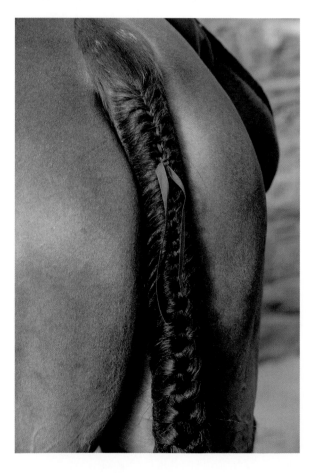

A red ribbon should be attached to the tail of a horse that may kick.

Plaiting

Hunters can be plaited using thread or bands. Thread looks smarter but bands are more practical as they take less time to do and can be easily taken out at the end of the day. (This can even be done whilst hacking back to the horsebox to save time later.) It used to be correct for hunters to have eleven or thirteen plaits down the neck with the forelock making an even number. These days this is not as important as plaiting to compliment the horse.

A full tail should be plaited and bandaged for the journey. A pulled tail should be dampened down and again plaited. If the horse is likely to soil the tail during travel, the whole length of the tail should be plaited and a second bandage applied to keep it clean. If conditions are wet and muddy, the tail can be plaited and taped up as for polo.

It is correct etiquette to tie a red ribbon in the tail of a horse that may kick. It is also useful to put one in the tail of ponies ridden by children. The red ribbon demands respect from other riders and they are less likely to use the pony as a stopping post. A green ribbon can be used on a young or inexperienced horse that may be nervous and require more space.

A hunter travelling tacked up. (Photo: Shannon Daly)

Grooming

On the morning of the hunt the horse should only require a quick flick over if he has been thoroughly groomed the night before. Stable stains should be removed and the eyes, nose and dock sponged. The feet can be picked out and oiled. Unlike at a competition, the final

A green ribbon is often seen on a young horse. (Photo: Shannon Daly)

Mounting at the meet. (Photo: Shannon Daly)

preparations can often not be done on arrival. It is quite common to have to park on a grass verge at the side of the road. For safety reasons it is beneficial to be able to unload and mount up as quickly as possible.

Many horses are often very excited when they arrive at a meet and for this reason it is common to travel with them already tacked up. Nosebands and girths can be tightened on arrival. Suitable rugs should be worn over the tack to prevent the horse getting cold.

A small travel grooming kit, sponge and water should be packed. Grey horses are most likely to need sponging off around the dock and hind legs. On arrival the tail bandages and rugs are removed and a final check is given before mounting.

The Master. (Photo: Shannon Daly)

A well turned-out hunter.

Care after hunting

There are several methods of caring for the horse after hunting, depending on the facilities available, the weather and how dirty the horse is. The most important factor to consider is the horse's welfare. He must be made warm and comfortable for the journey home, and once back in his own stable he should be thoroughly checked for any injury and settled down for the night.

If the weather is cold and the journey home not too long, the best option is to loosen the girth but leave the saddle on as it will help keep him warm during the journey. Put on a cooler such as a Thermatex. The bridle can be removed.

On returning home, put the horse in his stable and remove all the tack. Allow him to drink and have a roll. The worst of the sweat

Horses are saddled at the horsebox at point-to-points.

and mud can be washed off in warm water. The horse should be thoroughly checked over while doing so, paying particular attention to the legs, back and girth areas. A mild antiseptic wash can be added to the water. Scrape off excess water and apply a clean cooler and a warm stable rug. The legs should be towel dried and any cuts or scratches dealt with. The feet should be picked out and the shoes checked. If the horse looks comfortable and happy, he can be fed and left to settle.

Make another check on him later in the evening. Look over his general well-being, and feel down his legs for any heat or swelling. Check that he has eaten, had a drink and passed droppings as normal. The rugs should be changed or adjusted. Once happy, the horse can be left for the night.

The day after

The next morning the horse can be fed and left to eat. Any bandages should be removed at this stage. When he has finished eating, remove the rugs and make a thorough check over the horse in daylight. He may also be trotted up for soundness.

If necessary, give a quick flick over to remove any mud or sweat that was missed the night before. Any injuries should continue to be treated. It is usual to give the horse a day or more off after hunting. Turn him out in the paddock if possible or give him a gentle leg stretch in-hand or in a horse walker. The next day the horse should have a good hot cloth and thorough groom in readiness for the next day's hunting.

THE RACEHORSE AND POINT-TO-POINTER

Racing is a discipline that requires scrupulous management of every horse. Having a horse turn up to the racecourse in tiptop condition not only contributes to success but may also gain the groom the best-turned-out prize.

The racehorse is an athlete and is required to work hard to achieve high levels of fitness. Along with this can often come lameness and sore muscles. Daily grooming allows for such problems to be identified in the early stages and necessary treatment steps taken.

Daily management

Racing yards more often than not stable a greater number of horses than any other discipline. This obviously makes it a much more difficult task for the trainer to monitor each horse on a daily basis. For this reason the groom must take greater responsibility for the horse's well-being and be able to identify any problems early on. On a large racing yard each groom, commonly known as a lad or lass, will usually care for about four horses each. They are responsible for the mucking out, grooming and often the exercising of the horse. They usually accompany each horse to the races and are responsible for the turnout . This one-to-one relationship works well and a lad will often care for a horse throughout his whole racing career, forming a very special bond. For this reason working in racing can be very rewarding.

Clipping

During the winter months the horses will require clipping. The most common clips given are the hunter, chaser or high blanket. The normal clipping routine is generally followed, although thoroughbreds tend not to grow too much coat and may not need clipping as often as hunters. It is important to ensure that clipped horses are well rugged up, especially as thoroughbred horses feel the cold much more than heavier breeds do. Also, racing fitness will mean they don't carry any excess weight to help keep them warm. Failing to keep the horse warm enough will result in weight loss and reduced energy levels, which will most definitely result in poor performance. When choosing rugs, it is important to ensure that they fit well and are not going to rub. Thoroughbreds are often high at the withers and the rugs can dig in or rub at the shoulder. Putting on a lightweight sheet or cooler that fits snugly on the horse will help trap body heat. Thicker rugs can then be put on top or blankets can be used. It is often thought that putting on several layers is a better way of keeping warm than using one thick rug. The horse will also need a neck cover or blankets folded up the neck.

Grooming

On a daily basis the horse should be quartered before exercise. This ensures he is checked over and turned out smartly. After exercise he will need washing off or hot clothing, depending on how hot he is and the weather conditions. This gives a good opportunity to wash him while he is still warm and the pores open. Later in the day a more thorough groom is given. The horse is once again given a complete check-over of his legs, back and general condition. Often the trainer will inspect the horses at this time.

Trimming

Manes are pulled to a suitable length to plait or to lie over neatly if choosing not to plait. Similarly tails may be pulled or left full to plait. The tail is kept quite short and will be trimmed before racing.

Thoroughbreds are unlikely to grow much feather due to their breeding and it may not be necessary to trim. Whiskers and ears may be trimmed or left, depending on personal preference. A bridle path will help keep the mane comfortable and make it easier to put the bridle on, especially if the horse is highly strung.

Preparation for racing

The racehorse generally needs little extra preparation for a race day as the daily routine tends to keep the coat clean and prepared. Trimming can be done in the days leading up to a race, and the mane and tail washed if necessary. If the mane is not going to be plaited, it should be laid over in bunches the night before. A tail bandage should be used on a pulled tail.

Very little needs to be done to the horse before leaving for the races. It is usual to arrive about three hours before the race, giving ample time to prepare the horse once there. The horse will be allocated a stable in which to recover from the journey and settle. (Point-to-pointers are not given this luxury and will have to stay in the horsebox. For this reason, it is easier to prepare pointers before departure.)

Once settled, the horse can be groomed and prepared. Stable stains should be removed and white socks washed.

Plaiting

It is not compulsory to plait for racing. Some trainers believe that plaiting contributes to the horse's stress, which will be detrimental to performance. The more relaxed the horse stays, the more energy he conserves for the race. For this reason it is the policy on some yards that none of the horses is plaited, while others may plait the more relaxed types only. It may be felt that the horse is not in contention for the best-turned-out prize if he is not plaited.

The horse is given a thorough groom, and in winter it is essential that the horse is kept warm while this is being done. Quarter markings can be applied to suitable coats. The hooves should

Point-to-pointing.

The horse will need bathing after the race.

be picked out and oil applied when the horse leaves the stable. A bucket containing a brush, sponge and stable rubber can be taken to the saddling area to apply the final touches once the horse is saddled.

Care after the race

After the race the horse will be thoroughly washed to remove sweat and mud and to help cool him down in hot conditions. Racecourse stable yards are equipped with washdown areas and hosepipes, making the job much easier. The horse must be kept walking until a washdown area becomes available, and a rug may be needed to keep him warm. Care must be taken not to apply too much cold water over the back and hindquarters in cold weather as this can lead to muscle problems. After washing and scraping off the excess water, suitable rugs should be put on and the horse walked until he has fully recovered. Any injuries should be noted whilst washing and treated accordingly.

The following day routine checks should be made to ensure the horse is injury-free and is in good order.

13 Horse Health

Daily grooming provides an ideal opportunity to monitor the horse's health and condition. Identifying a problem in the early stages can prevent it becoming much more serious and in some cases spreading to other horses. Whether it is a quick brush off to tidy the horse before exercise or a thorough groom at the end of the day, it is a chance to observe and feel the skin, coat, legs and feet. It is also an opportunity to assess whether the horse is behaving in his normal manner. The skin and coat are major indicators of general health and well-being.

Like humans, every horse is different in his physical make-up and personality, and it is not until you are sufficiently familiar with the horse that small changes may be identified. When getting to know a horse it is important to note any lumps and bumps that may be the result of an old injury and are no longer active, and to be able to differentiate these from new injuries or ailments that need attention.

Monitoring the horse's weight and overall condition is a vital part of good management.

During grooming it should become second nature to check for signs of injury or ill-health. To do this properly requires knowledge of what is normal and what can be amiss. The best time to check the horse over is first thing in the morning before he leaves the stable.

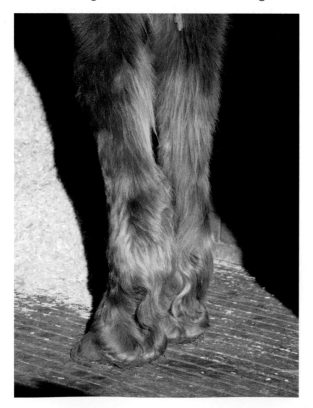

Two comments commonly heard when assessing a horse:

'Doesn't he look well? His coat has such a shine to it.'

and

'He looks very poor; his coat is dull and staring.'

Injuries are difficult to detect when the legs have lots of feather. (Photo: Shannon Daly)

SIGNS OF GOOD AND POOR HEALTH

On first approaching the horse in the stable or field, he should generally look bright, alert and responsive. There should be no obvious signs of lameness or discomfort. His eyes should be bright and free of discharge, and his nose clean and dry. Check that the corners and bars of the mouth are free from cuts and bruising, and that the mucous membranes of the gums are a salmon-pink colour and moist to the touch, not dry or tacky. Take note if the horse coughs in the stable or during exercise.

Check that the horse has eaten his food, as this may indicate problems with the teeth. Quidding is a problem that occurs when the horse is unable to chew his food effectively, often because his teeth are excessively sharp. Incorrect or partial chewing can lead to the horse spitting out a partially chewed bolus or clump of feed. This may appear as a rope of haylage, or parcel of partially chewed food material. Spilling grain may also be an indicator of oral discomfort, but can equally be normal for a very greedy horse. Foul-smelling breath is usually a sign of periodontal disease or infection. This may be within the mouth or in the airways. Older horses may also develop problems due to lost or broken teeth. Regular biannual visits from a qualified equine dental technician (EDT) should help prevent these problems. A list of qualified EDTs can be found at www.BAEDT.com. If these problems are ignored, the horse will lose condition and he will also be at risk of choke and impaction colic.

The horse should be carrying the right amount of condition for his level of fitness and the amount of work he is doing. It can often be difficult to notice subtle changes when observing the horse daily, but the use of a weigh tape weekly will ensure that these signs do not go unnoticed. It is important to train the eye to differentiate between a lean fit horse and one that is poor and underweight. Horses and ponies that are allowed to become overweight are also at risk of developing laminitis and putting undue stress on the cardiovascular system.

The coat should lie flat and have a healthy shine. This also applies to a horse living out at grass that is not being groomed daily. If the hair is standing on end, looking dull and staring, it is a sign that the horse is cold or unwell. The horse should not be seen shivering or sweating other than as a result of exercise or in hot weather.

The skin should be supple and elastic. When pinched on the neck, it should return to normal almost immediately; failure to do so is a sign of dehydration. This is a useful test following competition, travel or during illness. The skin should also be free from heavy scurf and grease. Abnormal changes in skin condition, itching, lumps or hair loss usually indicate a skin problem that requires attention.

The mane and tail should look healthy and not show signs of rubbing. Nor should there be any evidence of rubbing or soreness caused by ill-fitting tack or rugs.

The legs should be free of heat, swelling and pain on palpation. New injuries or leg problems are often accompanied by localized heat in the injured area. This is also likely to be sensitive to palpation and may cause lameness. Always compare one limb to the other as early clinical signs of a problem may be nothing more than a slight difference in temperature. Early recognition may prevent a mild injury becoming much more serious, especially if it is missed and the horse continues to be worked.

If a limb displays a more extensive swelling with a harder filling, accompanied by heat and lameness, it is usually an indicator of infection. This is obvious if the horse has a wound in the area. If there are signs of infection but no obvious injury, it may indicate a puncture wound. Such swelling is known as pitting oedema. If a finger is pressed to the tissue, the indent will remain for several seconds.

The wall of the hoof should be free of cracks and not too dry. The frog should not smell offensive and there should be no discharge. Both shod and bare feet should be regularly trimmed.

Droppings should be firm, formed balls that break on hitting the ground. Urine should not be dark in colour, nor contain blood. The horse should not struggle to pass urine.

The horse should display his usual characteristics when being groomed. A good-natured horse should not suddenly appear grumpy or uncomfortable, while a sharper horse should not be quiet and uninterested.

Eyes should be bright and free of discharge.

Pinching the skin to check for dehydration.

Checking the colour of the gums.

Legs should be free of heat, swelling and pain on palpation.

TEMPERATURE, PULSE AND RESPIRATION (TPR)

When signs of ill-health are noticed, it is important to assess the vital signs and to know what the normal range is for an adult horse at rest.

It is advisable to have an idea of each horse's normal TPR. This should be taken at rest, and the ideal time to do it is first thing in the morning before the horse has worked. This should be repeated over a period of five days and the averages worked out.

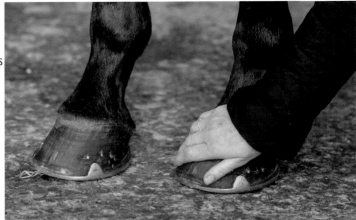

Feet ideally should be cool.

Temperature

The temperature can be taken using an equine or human thermometer. The digital equine is the easiest as it indicates when to take the reading. The horse must be tied up or held. The thermometer should be lubricated using Vaseline or saliva. Stand to the side of the horse to avoid being kicked. Raise the tail and insert the thermometer into the anus and then slightly angle it to one side. This places the probe against the gut wall and avoids inserting it into faeces, which may give a false reading. Leave in for a couple of minutes or until the thermometer indicates it is ready. Read and record the temperature. Always clean the thermometer before returning it to the first aid kit.

The temperature may raise through exercise, fear, pain, stress, excitement or infection.

Taking the temperature.

Pulse

The pulse can be taken by placing the index and ring fingers over an artery. The easiest artery to find is the maxillary. The best place to locate this is at the bottom of the lower jaw bone, just in front of where the heavy cheek muscles begin. Place your index and ring finger against the bottom of the mandible, and roll them around until you feel a cord-like structure slightly slimmer than a pencil. This bundle contains the vein, artery and associated nerve

---

TPR – NORMAL RESTING RATES

Temperature: 36.5 to 38.5 degrees centigrade
Pulse: 36 to 42 beats per minute
Respiration: 12 to 16 breaths per minute

which run together. Apply light pressure with the fingertips, gently pushing the artery against the jawbone until you locate the pulse. Count the beats for thirty seconds and then multiply by two to give the beats per minute.

The pulse will be higher in response to exercise, excitement, nervousness, high temperature, shock, pain, infection and any other stimulus. The resting pulse gets lower as the horse gets fitter.

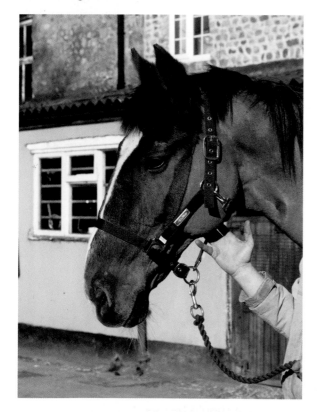

Taking the pulse. (Photo: Shannon Daly)

Respiration

The respiration rate is measured by counting the number of breaths a horse takes per minute, by observing his flanks moving in and out. It is important to note that one inhalation and exhalation counts as one breath. Count for thirty seconds and then double the number. It

is important that the horse remains still for this exercise.

The respiratory rate is increased by exercise, hot humid weather, excitement, pain, infection and other stimuli.

DERMATITIS

Dermatitis is the term for inflammation of the skin. This is quite common in horses and can be caused by allergies, fungal or bacterial infection, parasites, trauma and burns. Skin conditions are given specific names depending on the cause and the area of the body affected.

Often problems cannot be avoided but some conditions occur due to poor management or a lack of knowledge. It is therefore an advantage

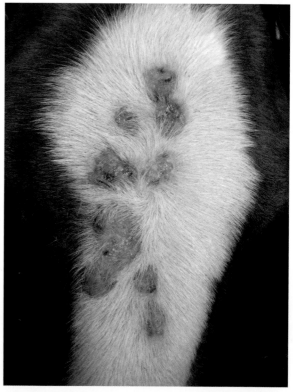

A nasty bacterial infection on the face. This might easily be confused with ringworm.

to recognize the symptoms of common skin disorders and to know how they arise, how they may be prevented and what treatments are available.

Ringworm

Causes

Ringworm is a common skin infection caused by a fungus. Transmission can be by direct contact with other infected animals, such as horses or cows, or via contaminated tack, rugs or grooming equipment. The fungus can also survive on hard structures such as stabling, fencing and horseboxes. Horses can carry the infection for up to three weeks without showing any symptoms, so it is easily spread before diagnosis. It appears more often when conditions are mild and damp.

Horses with a challenged immune system are more at risk of contracting ringworm. This includes young stock, older horses and horses that are under stress or harbouring a virus.

Symptoms

Small circular lesions appear on the skin, causing the hair to be slightly raised. The head, neck and flanks are the most commonly affected but it can be found anywhere. Eventually the hair will fall off, leaving a bald round patch. The skin will usually look dry and scurfy and the coat dull.

Treatment

Ringworm is self-limiting and, left untreated, it will eventually run its course but this can take from six to fifteen weeks. Therefore most owners want to treat it to minimize its impact on the routine of the yard.

If ringworm is at all suspected, it is advisable to treat immediately. All other horse owners

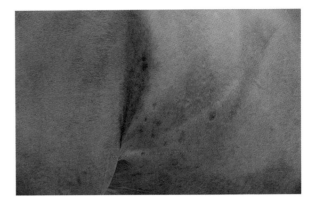
Scarring caused by ringworm.

and staff must be notified. If possible, isolate the affected horses, but if this is not an option a clear notice should be put on the stable door advising people not to touch the horse.

The vet will need to confirm the diagnosis and administer treatment. The most common treatment is a topical, anti-fungal solution that is applied to the lesions. This works more effectively if the scurfy skin and hair is removed first. This can be done by washing in a mild antiseptic. Make sure to keep all the equipment disinfected and use it only on horses showing symptoms.

Always complete a course of treatment, even if the condition appears to be better. Avoid grooming during this period as it will encourage the fungus to spread.

Use separate tools and rugs for affected horses while they are contagious. Virkon disinfectant should be used to disinfect any equipment that comes into contact with the horse. This should include the rider and groom's clothing. It should also be noted that ringworm can spread to humans so it is advisable to wear surgical gloves and dispose of them after use. If handling a number of horses, the infected ones should be dealt with last.

Affected horses are prohibited from racing and competing until the treatment is complete, followed by a nine to twelve day withdrawal period.

Prevention

Prevention is better than cure. If ringworm is suspected, always treat immediately. Avoid contact with other horses and ensure all equipment is kept separate and disinfected after use. New horses coming on to the yard should be thoroughly examined and, if possible, isolated for two to three weeks. The most susceptible animals are young stock or horses that have travelled on a commercial transporter and have come into contact with infected horses. Cattle also contract ringworm, so avoid turning horses out with cattle or near fencing where cattle have been.

Following an outbreak of ringworm, ensure that all equipment is thoroughly disinfected. Bedding should be completely changed and the stable thoroughly disinfected.

Once a horse has had ringworm it may develop an immunity to it for a period of time.

Rain scald, mud fever and cracked heels

Causes

Rain scald, mud fever and cracked heels are the same condition, but found in different areas on the body. It is a common infection caused by a bacteria called *Dermatophilus congolensis* that is present in the environment and activated by wet conditions. Horses living out without rugs on and standing in wet, muddy conditions are most at risk. Prolonged exposure to rain and mud causes the skin to become soft and vulnerable to superficial damage, allowing infection through this common organism. Grey and Palomino horses are more susceptible to rain scald, and white legs suffer more from mud fever and cracked heels.

Sometimes the condition may not be preventable, but poor management is often a contributing factor. It is also contagious and is often spread by sharing rugs, bandages and boots.

Symptoms

Rain scald appears mostly on the back and hindquarters but can also be seen on the neck. Scabs form under the hair, causing it to raise and feel bumpy. The scabs are often moist and weepy. If removed, they can leave painful, open sores.

Mud fever is similar and is found on the lower legs, most commonly at the back of the fetlock and pastern areas although it may spread higher. Failure to diagnose and treat the condition may lead to associated cellulitis, lymphangitis and lameness.

Cracked heels are a result of infection in the hollow of the pasterns. When the scabs fall off, they leave painful cracks. This leaves the horse susceptible to contamination and infection.

Scarring caused by rain scald.

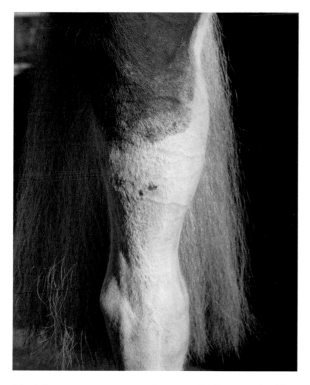

Mud fever can occur anywhere on the legs, and white socks are more prone to it. (Photo: Shannon Daly)

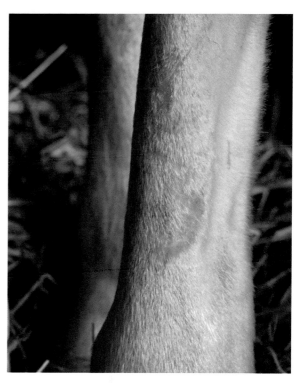

These legs have recovered from mud fever. (Photo: Shannon Daly)

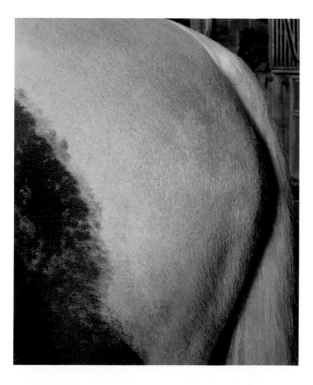

Treatment

The first point of action is to remove the cause. If the horse is living out, he should be brought into a dry, clean stable. The scabs should be removed using an antibacterial shampoo and thoroughly dried afterwards. It may be necessary to clip the area if the hair is preventing effective treatment. It must be remembered, however, that feather offers protection to the leg in wet and muddy conditions so excess trimming should be avoided if the horse is going to be turned out once treatment is finished. Apply antibacterial cream or gel to the area twice daily. This treatment should be continued until the skin appears healthy again.

The hindquarters show scars from rain scald. (Photo: Shannon Daly)

Bandaging should be avoided. The bacteria thrives on a lack of oxygen, so allowing air to the skin will help heal the condition more quickly.

Never try to pick dry, stubborn scabs as this will cause deeper wounds and soreness. Hard scabs can be softened by using warm water and antibacterial wash. If necessary, for really stubborn scabs, apply a cleansing ointment and then cover the affected area with cling film and bandage for an hour or two. The scabs should then soften and be easily removed.

In severe cases, where there is inflammation and lameness, it will be necessary to call the vet as the infection is likely to require antibiotics. Veterinary advice should also be sought if the condition is not responding to treatment or is spreading.

Avoid turning the horse out or working him in wet muddy conditions until the infection has cleared.

Prevention

- Rug up when turning out in rain for long periods of time.
- Avoid using equipment that has been worn by infected horses.
- Avoid turning out in heavily poached paddocks. If the horse has a tendency to stand in muddy gateways, try to fence this area off or put down some hardcore to improve drainage.
- Daily checks of horses that are living out during the winter will ensure early diagnosis of a problem and prevent it from spreading.
- Keep the legs clean and dry but avoid over-washing and scrubbing as this can often cause further problems.
- Pig oil or a mud fever barrier cream, such as udder cream, can be applied daily to dry clean legs. This offers protection and helps prevent problems.

Folliculitis.

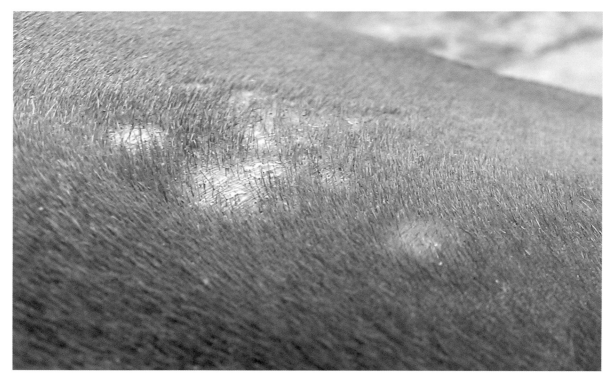

The scabs are removed.

- Identifying and treating any small cuts and nicks on the limbs will help prevent infection taking hold.
- Disinfect all equipment that has had contact with infected areas.
- Horses do not build up immunity to the problem. On the contrary, horses that are prone to the condition are more likely to get it regularly if preventive measures are not taken.

Folliculitis

Causes

Folliculitis is a bacterial infection of the hair follicles. It is caused when dirt and bacteria enter open pores, causing infection in the area, which is often transmitted during exercise when the horse becomes warm. The condition is more likely to occur if the saddle pad is dirty, the coat is very greasy or the saddle moves about causing friction. It can also occur if a horse is rugged up using dirty rugs when he is still hot after work.

It may also be seen after clipping, caused by a blade rash.

Symptoms

Small nodules appear, most commonly in the saddle or girth area but also in other places. The nodules are usually hot and sensitive to touch. There may be some inflammation around them, especially if friction is the cause. The nodules will form scabs which can weep and discharge pus.

Treatment

Remove the cause so that the condition is not prolonged. Wash the affected area with an antiseptic wash and allow it to dry completely before applying dry, clean rugs. In more severe cases, where the condition is spreading or infection occurs, call the vet. The horse will require an oral antibiotic and daily topical treatment.

If the problem is under the saddle or in the girth area, the horse should not be ridden while the infection is present as it may cause him discomfort.

Prevention

Keep the skin and coat as clean as possible. Wash the saddle area with a mild Dettol solution after exercise, and do not apply rugs until the area is dry. Use only clean numnahs and rugs. Ensure the saddle fits correctly.

Sunburn

Causes

Sunburn occurs when unprotected skin is exposed to ultraviolet light. The pigmentation in the skin offers some natural protection but non-pigmented horses with white or pink skin are extremely vulnerable to damage. It commonly affects horses and ponies that are living out or have been turned out for long periods during the summer months and have no form of shade or protection. It doesn't take long for the skin to burn, so it can also happen during exercise or when standing in the show ring.

Sometimes horses develop inexplicable signs of sunburn. This can be due to photosensitization and can affect both non-pigmented and lightly pigmented skin. Photosensitizers are found in plants such as buttercups and cow parsley, which commonly grow in paddocks and hedgerows, and are easily absorbed around the muzzle when grazing, resulting in sunburn symptoms.

Symptoms

The muzzle, eyes and heels are the most commonly affected areas as the skin is often pink and has very little hair for protection. The skin will initially look very pink and sore. It will then dry out and peel or blister. The new skin will be more vulnerable to burning.

Treatment

Bring the horse in out of the sun. Bathe the affected area using a very dilute antiseptic wash, removing any dead skin. Dry the area and apply wound cream or gel if necessary. Severe burns may blister and become infected. Veterinary treatment will then be necessary.

The horse should not be exposed to sunlight until the condition has totally healed.

Prevention

Fields should provide some form of shelter or shade. If the horse is susceptible, apply high-factor sun cream before turning out or exercise. It may also be necessary to use sun cream on stabled horses if their heads come over the door in unshaded areas.

If the horse is living out, it is necessary to apply the cream several times a day. Masks can also be worn to offer some protection.

Allergies, Urticaria and Hives

Causes

- Bedding
- Feed
- Weeds and plants
- Medication
- Inhaled pollen or mould
- Fly bites or stings
- Washing detergents
- Topical washes

- Heat
- Heavy exercise

Symptoms

Lesions appear under the skin. They can vary from small spots to larger weals, welts and lumps, ranging from 1cm to 20cm across. They have a raised, flat-topped appearance. It can take minutes or hours for the rash to develop. The most common place for them to appear is on the neck and shoulder, but they can cover the whole body and legs. In severe cases they are also found on the mucous membranes of the mouth, nose, eyes, rectum and vagina.

The lumps often cause no pain and the horse is blissfully unaware of the condition. In some cases the skin may feel hot and itchy. The horse may also appear excited or restless.

Treatment

If possible, identify the cause and remove it immediately. In some cases this may be obvious, perhaps following a change in management, such as new feed or bedding, or following a treatment. If the horse comes in from the field with the condition it is worth walking round the paddock to look for the possible culprit. Often it can be a plant found growing in the hedgerow. Sometimes, however, the cause is not obvious.

Most cases spontaneously resolve in one or two days and do not require treatment. During this period keep the skin cool and do not over-rug.

If symptoms persist, the horse shows signs of stress or the condition is worsens, call the vet immediately.

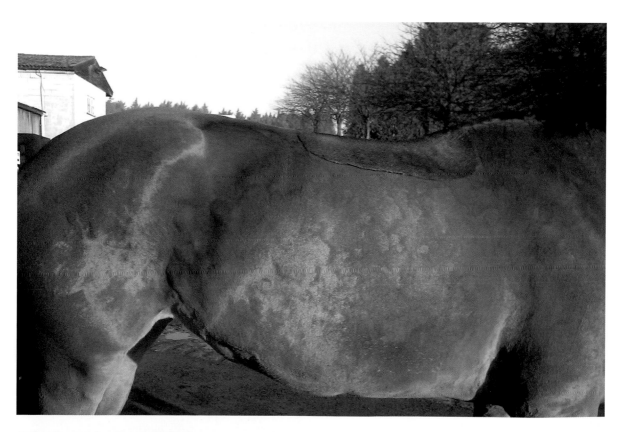

Urticaria covering the whole body.

Prevention

Prevention is only possible once the cause has been identified. A process of elimination can be used to rule out all possible causes if the condition repeats itself.

Good stable management will help.

Sweet itch

Cause

Sweet itch is caused by an allergic reaction to the saliva of midges. It occurs more frequently when horses are attacked by midges in the paddock but can also happen when stabled. Around 5 per cent of horses are affected.

Symptoms

Midges tend to bite the mane area and the top of the tail, but in severe cases the problem is more widespread. The allergic reaction causes extreme itchiness, resulting in the horse rubbing vigorously on anything available. He may roll, pace excessively and seek mutual grooming from field companions. The symptoms are worse at dawn and dusk when the midges are particularly active.

The rubbing will cause hair from the mane and tail to be lost, and the skin becomes dry and flaky, often leading to open sores, exacerbated by rubbing. These sores are susceptible to infection. Over time the horse may become lethargic or ultra-sensitive to the areas being touched.

Once the allergy has developed, it tends to stay with the horse for life. The condition is present during spring, summer and autumn, with winter the only season to offer some respite.

Treatment

Unfortunately, there is no cure for sweet itch but the problem can be managed to reduce the discomfort and stress to the horse.

Midges are more likely to be present in a warm, damp environment, so avoid turning out on marshy, wooded or clay land. An exposed field is more suitable. The horse may also be attacked by midges in the stable if it is in close proximity to the muck heap.

Avoid turning out at dawn or dusk when the midges are at their worst. The top door of the stable can be closed at these times to offer some protection and prevent the horse rubbing on the door frame.

Insect repellents can be applied but they rarely offer sufficient protection. Deet is the most common active ingredient in fly repellents, but most contain only around 20 per cent. The National Sweet Itch Centre recommends that Deet close to 100 per cent strength is effective in giving up to six hours' protection.

Benzyl benzoate is commonly used and can be easily obtained. The affected area should be washed and dried before the lotion is applied. It should be thoroughly worked into the mane and the dock, but care should be taken not to apply it to broken skin. Application should commence as soon as midges start to appear and not wait until the horse has started rubbing.

Greasy and oily surfaces repel midges. Application of medical liquid paraffin may help but this tends to be quite messy and is not ideal if the horse is being ridden. Some substances may cause an allergic reaction so it is advisable to do a small skin test before using extensively.

Steroid creams and soothing lotions can be applied to reduce inflammation and offer some relief to irritated areas, but it must be remembered that these do not prevent midge attack. The use of antihistamines may offer some relief but can cause undesirable side-effects. The vet may administer Corticosteroids by injection. This may bring temporary relief but in time it becomes less effective.

There are many rugs available that

Midges will be worse if muck is piled up close to the stables. (Photo: Shannon Daly)

offer protection from ear to tail. The most highly recommended is the Boett, which differs from other brands as it is made from a unique purpose-designed fabric that midges cannot bite through. It is tough but lightweight and can be worn in and out of the stable.

Prevention

Sweet itch cannot be prevented. Managing the condition as discussed is the best that can be done.

Bio Plus capsules, given weekly, are said to help treat a faulty immune system. The treatment should start during the winter, before the sweet itch becomes a problem. Cavalesse is a vitamin-based supplement that improves the quality of the skin and can help with many skin issues.

Avoid buying a horse that is known to suffer from sweet itch, or shows any signs of it, as it can be as distressing for the owner as it is for the horse. It is also difficult to compete with a horse with sweet itch and showing is most certainly compromised.

PARASITIC INFECTIONS

Mites and mange

Causes

Mites are tiny insects, so small they cannot be seen with the naked eye. They live on the skin surface or just beneath it and cause intense itchiness. If not treated, the mites will reproduce continuously, and the horse's condition will deteriorate.

There are three species of mite that mainly affect the horse:

- *Psoroptic Mites* are found in the mane and tail. They cause rubbing and hair loss, and the skin underneath appears dry and flaky. The horse may be prone to head shaking. The condition is commonly referred to as mange.
- *Sarcoptes Mites* attack the body, neck and head, causing the horse to rub these areas. The hair can be lost and extreme rubbing often creates open wounds that are prone to secondary infection.
- *Chorioptic Mites* are found on the lower legs and cause the horse to stamp his feet and chew at his legs. The condition can lead to mud fever as bacteria can enter the bite sites. It can be identified by bald patches behind the knees. Horses with heavy feather are more susceptible to the condition.

Treatment

The vet should be called to confirm diagnosis and prescribe treatment. This usually takes the form of a topical anti-parasitic solution. The hair may need to be clipped to treat the problem effectively, especially in the case of heavy feathers. The whole of the horse should be treated as the mites can migrate around the body. Any secondary infection should be treated accordingly.

It is important to treat all horses that have been in contact with the infected animal. The bedding should be totally removed and all rugs and equipment washed in Virkon disinfectant.

Prevention

Mites can be spread by direct or indirect contact. When possible, isolate the affected horse; keep his equipment separate and disinfect it after use. Avoid using stables where infected horses have been until the bedding has been changed.

Lice

Cause

Lice are tiny parasitic insects that live on the hair and coat of animals. They are usually species specific. Any horse can be infested, even with the best care and management. Sharing clothing and equipment spreads the problem, along with direct contact. Lice tend to survive better in a longer coat, and are more commonly found on horses that have a weak immune system due to age, illness or poor management.

The lice either suck the blood or feed off the skin. The sucking type is typically found on the mane and tail and above the hooves, while the biting type tends to be found on areas with shorter hair. Both will cause the horse to itch and rub, resulting in hair loss and sores. If not treated, the infestation will worsen and can result in the horse becoming run-down.

Lice and eggs can be seen in the hair. Sucking lice are grey in colour, while the biting ones are brownish.

Treatment

Topical powder can be bought off the shelf but is not always successful in treating the condition. Prescription medicine is more effective.

All clothing and equipment should be washed in Virkon disinfectant.

Prevention

Isolate any affected horses and keep their equipment separate. Regularly check for any signs of lice when grooming and always thoroughly examine any new horses when they arrive on the yard.

Pinworms

Causes

The horse ingests the eggs through grazing, feeding or mutual grooming. Once ingested, the eggs hatch into larvae which feed off the mucosal lining of the intestine. Mature females pass out through the rectum and anal area, laying their eggs under the tail.

Symptoms

The main indication of pinworm infestation is tail rubbing, causing similar symptoms to sweet itch. The coat may also be rubbed at the point of buttock, causing open sores. The horse may appear agitated, kicking out with his hind legs.

On closer examination eggs may be seen around the anus. If the problem is not diagnosed after a period of time, the horse will lose condition and look poor.

Treatment

Remove all the eggs and thoroughly cleanse all affected areas with a mild disinfectant. Treat any secondary infection. Seek advice from the vet on a suitable worming programme.

Thoroughly disinfect all equipment and clothing. Remove bedding and disinfect the stable.

Prevention

Regular appropriate worming and good pasture management should control the problem. Thoroughly check the horse for symptoms when grooming, and examine any new horses entering the yard.

SKIN GROWTHS

Sarcoids

Causes

Sarcoids are commonly occurring skin tumours that can develop anywhere on the horse's skin. Although they are a type of cancer, they do not spread to the internal organs.

The cause of sarcoids is not yet fully understood, though it is thought that the skin may be more prone to the development of a sarcoid if it has previously suffered trauma. Once a horse has developed one, more are likely to appear.

Symptoms

There are six broad classifications for equine sarcoids. They vary greatly in size and shape and in how they grow. They have a tendency to appear more on geldings than on mares, and can develop anywhere but are more commonly found on the face, chest, girth, groin and sheath.

Sarcoids can be aggravated by trauma, such as a direct blow or rubbing. If the top is knocked off, it becomes open to infection.

Treatment

Unfortunately, as yet there is no treatment available that offers guaranteed success in treating sarcomas. A sarcoid that has been treated may reappear and the horse will be more prone to others occurring.

Initially it is advisable to monitor each sarcoid but take no further action unless it is in an area that causes a problem from interference. Advice should also be sought if the sarcoid grows or changes in appearance. The vet will assess it and suggest how best to treat it. This can often be a costly and lengthy process.

Prevention

Sarcoids cannot be prevented. It is advisable to seriously consider avoiding purchasing a horse that has any history of the problem.

Warts

Causes

Warts are caused by the Equine Papilloma Virus. They are commonly found on young stock but rarely in mature horses. They are spread from one horse to another by direct contact and indirectly via equipment.

Symptoms

Warts are most commonly seen on the nostrils and muzzle but also appear around the eyes or other areas where the hair is fine. They are small irregular bumps, greyish in colour, which often appear quite suddenly and can be in small or large quantities. They are usually pain free and do not cause a problem. However, occasionally they may crack and bleed, resulting in a secondary infection.

Treatment

Treatment is not usually necessary as warts tend to disappear spontaneously after a few months as the horse builds up a resistance to the virus. If this is not the case, veterinary advice should be sought.

Prevention

There is no prevention against warts but it is possible to control the spread from one horse to another by keeping horses and equipment separate.

Girth galls

Causes

A girth gall is caused by the girth rubbing the skin. It commonly occurs when horses are brought back into work after a holiday as the skin becomes very soft. It may also be caused by a badly fitting girth or a reaction to the material of the girth. Failure to keep the girth area clean will predispose this area to sores.

Symptoms

The gall can be an open or closed sore. The area most commonly affected is behind the elbow and it typically appears as a small swelling. The hair may show signs of friction. If this goes unnoticed, or is not acted upon, the hair will be lost and an open sore will develop. The area will feel warm and be sensitive to the touch. The horse may show signs of aggression when being groomed and saddled, and may take shorter steps when being ridden.

Treatment

Identify and remove the cause. If the gall is closed, the area should be left without a girth until the swelling has subsided and the sensitivity has gone. If the wound is open, it should be cleaned and exposed to fresh air to help with healing. Girths should not be used until the soreness has gone from the skin.

Prevention

Before bringing the horse back into work after a break, ensure his coat and skin are clean. Saline solution can also be applied to help harden the skin. Always thoroughly wash off sweaty areas after work, followed by grooming when the coat has dried.

An old saddle sore. The hair has grown back white. (Photo: Shannon Daly)

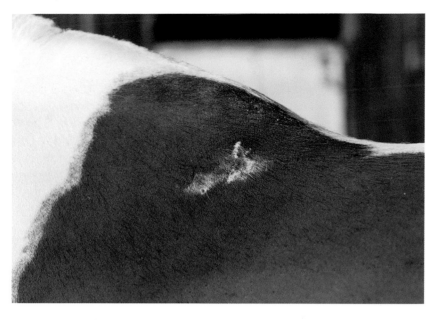

Use the correct sized girth for the horse. Some girths are shaped to help prevent rubbing behind the elbow areas. A fleecy girth cover can be used on particularly sensitive horses.

Saddle sores

Saddle sores may be caused by ill-fitting saddles, dirty skin or saddle pads and unbalanced riding. The most common sites for sores are on either side of the withers or where the back of saddle sits. If the saddle is too tight, it will put pressure on the withers, but if it is too loose and moves about it can cause friction under the seat. Initially the skin may not be broken. It is essential to run the hands along the back when grooming to feel for swellings and sensitivity. It should also be noted if the hair is looking rubbed. Failing to notice these early signs may result in a more serious problem. Saddle sores should be treated as for girth galls. If the hair is lost it can often grow back white due to the damaged hair follicles. This is commonly seen at the withers.

Foot problems

Care of the feet is one of the most important aspects of grooming and the feet and shoes should be checked daily as part of the grooming routine. Failure to recognize when the farrier is needed or that the feet are not in good health may result in lameness.

Most horses need shoeing every six weeks. Horses with problem feet may only last four weeks, while the riding horse or pony may last longer. The feet grow more quickly in summer than in winter, so the cycle may vary during the year.

SIGNS THAT THE HORSE NEEDS THE FARRIER

- The toe is too long. If wearing shoes, the wall may start to protrude.
- Risen clenches.
- Lost, loose or twisted shoes.
- Worn shoes.
- Lameness.

The farrier is required every four to six weeks. (Photo: Shannon Daly)

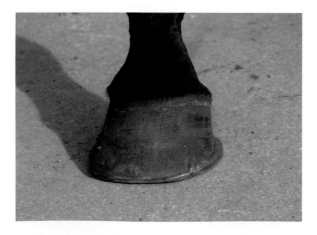

The clenches are risen and the foot is growing over the shoe. (Photo: Shannon Daly)

Signs of a healthy foot

The following should be noted when picking out the feet:

● All four feet should feel roughly the same temperature. Cold feet are ideal but on hot days it is natural that the feet will feel warm. If only one foot is hot, it is usually an indicator of a problem. The affected foot should be checked for obvious causes such as a stone and the horse trotted up to check for soundness.
● The wall of the hoof should appear healthy and free from cracks. It should not be too dry and should have a naturally polished surface.
● The sole of the foot should be concave and not show signs of bruising.
● The frog should be well defined. In wet conditions it will feel rubbery and in dry conditions it will be hard. Signs of discharge or an offensive odour are indicators of thrush. Care should be taken when using the hoof pick around the frog as it is a sensitive structure.

Thrush

Thrush is a common bacterial infection of the frog.

Causes

The main cause is poor stable management, which includes not picking the feet out regularly and the horse left standing for long periods on soiled bedding. Horses with contracted heels or deep clefts are more prone to thrush as this makes it more difficult to clean out the feet properly.

Symptoms

The main symptom is a strong offensive odour coming from the frog, often accompanied by a dark discharge. The foot will appear moist and will often crumble away when the hoof pick is used. The horse may be sensitive to having his feet picked out and in some cases may be lame.

Treatment

Remove the cause. The horse should be kept on clean, dry bedding. Scrub the feet daily in Virkon disinfectant until all signs of infection are gone. Cotton wool soaked in iodine can be plugged into deep clefts to keep them clean and protected.

Prevention

Pick out the feet at least once a day and always after work and turning out. Horses that are prone to thrush should have their feet scrubbed two or three times a week. Regular visits from the farrier to keep the frog tidy and dress the feet will help keep the foot healthy.

Wound management

Basic wound management can save time and money. Identifying a wound and knowing the appropriate treatment can prevent infection and secondary problems. Wounds

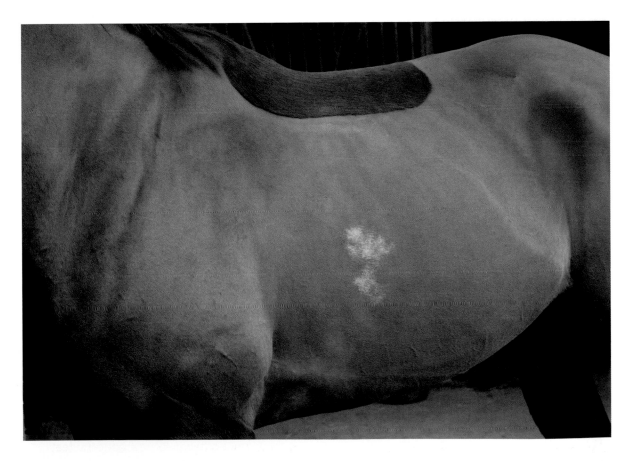

Hair often grows back white after injury. (Photo: Shannon Daly)

frequently become infected. Often a severe-looking wound heals much more quickly and is less complicated than one that initially looks superficial. The type of wound, where it is sited and its treatment are all things to be considered.

Types of wound

An *incision* is a cleanly cut wound or slice, usually caused by a sharp object. Such wounds often bleed quite heavily, and are usually good candidates for suturing, stapling or gluing.

GUIDELINES FOR TREATING WOUNDS

- Assess the wound and the overall condition of the horse. There may be other injuries that are not as obvious and the horse may be in shock, requiring immediate veterinary attention.
- Control excessive bleeding by applying direct pressure to the wound. If possible, use a sterile dressing and an elastic bandage. The vet should be called immediately and the dressing kept in place until he arrives. If the wound continues to bleed, more dressings should be applied on top.
- If veterinary attention is required, it is a question of the sooner the better. The wound can be cleaned but avoid putting on any cream, gel or powder before the vet arrives.
- Always call the vet if bleeding is excessive, if sutures are required, if there is significant lameness, or if the wound cannot be cleaned effectively and if there is a risk of infection.
- It is especially important to seek veterinary advice if the wound is in the region of a joint, as joint infections can be extremely serious.
- Always call the vet in the case of a puncture wound.
- If the vet is not required, clean the wound and apply appropriate treatment and a dressing if necessary.
- Trim the hair around the wound prior to cleaning. Before doing this, put a small amount of wound gel on to the wound to prevent hair contamination.
- Clean the wound using warm water and a saline solution. Use a new piece of cotton wool each time you go to the solution. Continue until all the debris is removed and the wound looks clean. Flushing with a larger syringe, using dilute saline, is also extremely helpful.
- An Animalintex poultice can be applied overnight as a last resort to clean the wound. Avoid using the poultice if possible as it creates a perfect environment for bacteria to thrive, and never use one on a joint.
- Apply wound gel or cream.
- Avoid powders completely and sprays initially. Spray can be used as a barrier when the wound is healing.
- A dry dressing may be applied if the wound looks susceptible to infection.
- Keep the wound dry and clean.
- Check that the horse has been vaccinated against tetanus. If not, the vet will need to administer a booster.
- Call the vet if a leg wound starts to look infected, the leg becomes hot and inflamed or the horse goes lame.

A *laceration* is a tear, often caused by wire. Lacerations are not easy to suture due to the torn rough edges of skin, often with underlying soft tissue damage. There is a greater risk of infection due to contamination.

Abrasions are minor skin wounds requiring minimal treatment.

A *puncture* is a penetrating wound that can appear superficial on the surface but can cause significant trauma beneath. There is a high risk of infection through contamination. Often the skin will heal before the internal structures.

Wound Treatment

Treatment will vary depending on the severity and nature of the wound. The main goal is to decrease the risk of infection and secondary problems.

FIRST AID KIT

An up-to-date first aid kit should be kept on the yard and in the horsebox or trailer for use at competitions. They should be kept locked away with an inventory.

There are legal requirements concerning what can be stored and administered without veterinary assistance.

Contents

- Non-woven Gamgee
- Assortment of elastic bandages
- Cohesive bandages such as Vet Wrap
- Elastoplast bandage
- Various sterile dressings
- Cotton wool
- Ear buds
- Elastoplast roll
- Duct tape
- Clingfilm
- Animalintex poultice
- Kaolin poultice
- Hibiscrub
- Pevadine
- Hexocil
- Savlon
- Cleansing creams
- Antiseptic cream and gel
- Wound spray
- Surgical spirit
- Dettol
- Epsom salts
- Vaseline
- Lip salve
- Sun screen
- Fly repellent
- Electrolytes
- Thermometer
- Scissors
- Tweezers
- Twitch
- Syringes
- Sterile bowl
- Sterile bucket
- Tubbing bucket
- Equiboot
- Ice packs
- Disposable gloves
- Clean towels
- Disposable cloths
- Tape

14 Traditional versus Modern Grooming

Care of the horse has changed a great deal over the last twenty-five years. Traditional grooming is carried out less frequently, while both turnout and fashions in some disciplines have moved away from the look of the past. There are disadvantages and advantages to both traditional and modern approaches. This chapter explains and discusses the reasons for this change in the horse world.

STABLE MANAGEMENT

In general, overall standards are continuously improving in all areas of horse care. What we feed our horses has changed through better knowledge and research into nutrition. The condition of the horse has improved immensely as a result of this. Most compound feeds now have a much higher oil content, which gives the skin and coat a natural healthy appearance.

Whether it is a private horse owner or a large commercial yard, less time is spent grooming the horse in the traditional manner. The main reasons for this are to do with changes in lifestyle, finances and time. Private horse owners often have to juggle caring for their horse with work and family commitments. It has therefore become much more common to put the horse in a commercial yard on full or part livery. Often the owner will only be able to ride the horse once or twice during the week, spending more time with him at the weekends. Although this may not compromise the care of the horse, the owner is not able to build up as much of a partnership with him.

Nowadays commercial yards provide a good service and horses are very well cared for. However, thorough grooming does not often take priority in the daily routine. Modern facilities with washboxes, equipped with hot and cold water and heat lamps, have also changed how things are done. Such facilities make it possible to bath a horse all year round. Often horses are taken to the washbox immediately after work, bathed, dried off and rugged up. The advantage of this is that the horse can be checked over for injury and soreness. From a cleanliness point of view, the horse does not require grooming later that day. The disadvantage is that often soreness, heat and swellings do not always appear immediately after work. Traditionally horses were cooled, rugged up and put away after work and a thorough groom would be done several hours later, by which time injuries would be apparent. Bathing reduces the amount of labour needed but still ensures the horse is clean and checked for health problems. It does not, however, allow the groom to spend enough time with the horse.

The question that has to be asked is 'Have standards dropped due to this change in management?' Observing a show horse that has been produced for the ring, the answer would have to be 'No.'

A physiotherapist treating a horse. (Photo: Shannon Daly)

In showing, horses are turned out to a much higher standard than ever before and this is partly due to the use of a wide range of products. For example, a coat enhancer can certainly produce in minutes as good – or better – a result as hours of grooming.

Traditionally a thorough groom would be given daily, lasting around forty minutes. Two or three times per week the horse would also be strapped, spending a further thirty minutes working on the muscles. These days horses are routinely checked out by an equine physiotherapist. After treatment the groom is often given exercises to treat the horse daily. Again this is an advantage to the horse but may take up some of the time allotted for grooming. In other cases the physiotherapist may recommend the use of a muscle stimulator or magnetic rug. This again requires time that otherwise may have been spent on grooming.

Clipping trends have changed over the years. It used to be that only horses in hard work were given a full or hunter clip. Those in lighter to medium work would have had a trace or blanket clip. Both of these require much more grooming than a full clip. It has to be said that a fully clipped-out horse that is hot clothed daily looks the smarter of the two and is much more labour-saving – but again the time is often not spent with the horse to improve basic handling and manners.

The quality of rugs available now has also improved. They help to lay the coat much better so often the body does not appear to need grooming. Neck covers and rugs are frequently used in and out of the stable. These offer more protection from the cold and prevent the horse getting too muddy when turned out in the field. It used to be necessary to give a thorough groom to a horse that had been turned out due to the amount of mud on him. These days it is usually only the legs that are muddy and more often than not they are simply hosed off rather than being left to dry and then groomed. The neck covers and hoods, if put on correctly, also assist in laying the mane. This reduces the amount of time required to put the mane into plaits or bunches.

Showjumping fashions have changed.

All disciplines follow a dress code for both horse and rider.

In some respects the care and treatment of horses today will produce a higher standard of turnout on the outside but often at the expense of the precious time spent developing the partnership that will enable the recognition of subtle changes in the horse's mental and physical state

FASHION

All disciplines follow a dress code for horse and rider. Traditionally for the horse it was a matter of plain and simple tack. The rider's dress code varied slightly between disciplines and levels within disciplines. Today the rider's attire and the horse's tack have become quite varied and very discipline-specific.

In the hunting and eventing worlds there have been few changes. In the lower levels of competition and for autumn hunting riders wear tweed. Moving up the levels, the turnout of the horse is expected to be of a higher level and riders wear navy or black coats. Tack has remained relatively plain, although a wider variety of bits is seen and the design of saddles has changed. This is more in the interest of the horse's well-being and the rider's effectiveness then a fashion statement.

In contrast, dressage and showjumping have moved away from their traditional ways, creating more of an individual look. The turnout of dressage horses remains at a very high standard, and even at the lower levels most horses are still plaited. Plaiting trends have varied over the years, often taking ideas from the continent, such as wrapping white tape around the plaits, although this is not often seen these days. Tack and equipment are often more extravagant: for example, many horses wear brow bands with bling even at the higher levels. As for the riders, subtle changes have been made in style and more effort is made to look elegant.

Showjumping has gone through the biggest change for both horse and rider, perhaps because it is a high-profile sport that gains a great deal of media attention. The most notable change in the turnout of the horse is the lack of plaiting, even at top levels of competition. This is due to the fact that the showjumping world is often far more hectic than other disciplines and it has become acceptable not to plait. Horses are still cared for and turned out to a high standard. The tack and equipment worn often has much more glitter and bling. Fashions for the rider have dramatically changed. Jackets are more fitted and most colours are acceptable. It is now compulsory to wear hats with a chin strap, which has led to them becoming more attractive and sleek. Riding boots are more slender and fitted. The overall picture of the rider is much more glamorous. Traditionalists

may not approve of this modern look but the glamour may bring more interest to the sport which benefits it financially.

In the quality of turnout the showing world has changed the most by far. This is without a doubt due to the use of the products now available. The dress code for the rider may not have changed but it has become more stylish. The turnout of the horse has improved dramatically. Some people do not approve as the look at times can be overdone and appears too artificial. There is a fine line between getting it right and going over the top.

Racing and hunting are probably the disciplines that remain the most traditional in care and turnout. Although racing is a very high-profile sport and is televised much more than other disciplines, jockeys and owners rarely adopt a glamorous approach. The financial backing in racing enables the horses to be cared for in a more traditional manner.

As with all things in life, the way in which horses are cared for will continue to change. It is hoped that this will result in a better knowledge of management, leading to improved performance and happy horses. Along with this, it is also my hope that people will continue to spend quality time grooming and caring for their horses to build up a relationship that will prove to be rewarding and enjoyable for both.

Index

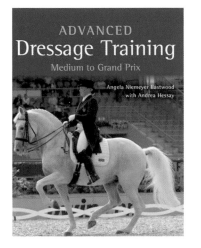

978 1 78500 088 1

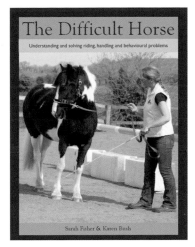

978 1 84797 427 3

978 1 84797 301 6

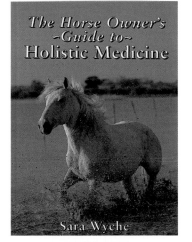

978 1 85223 942 8

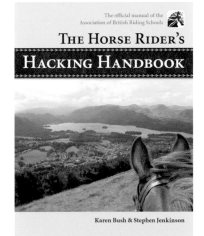

978 1 84797 285 9

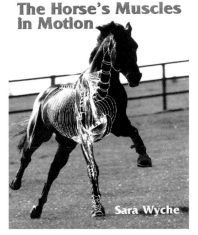

978 1 86126 456 5

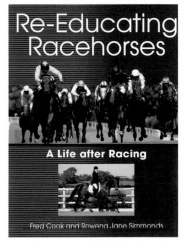

978 1 84797 253 8

978 1 84797 233 0

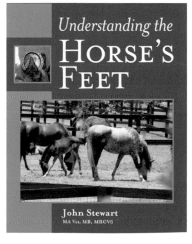

978 1 84797 476 1